7
WHEN ᴜᴜ ι ɾ CALLS

"What was a mother of five doing here in a combat zone?" COL Carol Rogers (RET) asks herself this at the opening of her gripping memoir, which chronicles her unlikely journey from struggling single mother to high-ranking Army Intelligence Colonel in wartime Iraq. Her accounts are detailed and vivid; you feel alongside Rogers as she takes her first terrifying jumps out of a plane (while her kids watch!) or witnesses the birth of a grandchild. With striking honesty and vulnerability, she delves into her conflicting feelings of pride and guilt at her successes at work and failures at home, sometimes questioning if it was all worth it. Roger's story is as relatable as it is awe-inspiring. Whether you are a working parent, a single serviceman, or a student of history, *When Duty Calls* is a must-read.

Rena Marie Pacella, Former military-tech writer and editor at *Popular Science Magazine*

Airborne, All the Way, COL Rogers! Carol's book and story confirm why so many of us sought her out for mentorship and guidance as we sought our way forward. Her book depicts so many examples of tenacity, persistence, and demand for equality, making it a must-read for us all to live by. Any young officer, male or female, who reads this will be inspired to never quit or accept "you can't" for an answer. I was impressed with her before, but after reading this book, I see all the challenges, personal and professional, she overcame to be such a great inspiration to all of us and for her children to emulate.

MG Robert L. Walter, Jr., US Army (RET), Member of Board of Directors for G2K Labs and Halo Privacy

True Grit. These are the words that come to mind after reading this story of a woman who accepted no limits and knew no bounds. With tenacious determination, she courageously pursued her dreams and desires to live a life of mission and purpose with the US Army.

Our nation's military and intelligence division is in a better place because of her vision and commitment to conduct herself, her units, and her command in a spirit of excellence. From the Reserves to the Pentagon and across the world, Carol lived out her honor throughout the 32 years of service she gave to our country, impacting the lives of all those around her. She left her mark of leadership and innovative logistics in military intelligence throughout her service, most notably at Abu Ghraib, Saddam Hussein's "death camp" in Iraq. Carol endured life-threatening and primitive conditions and hardships all along the way, but her persistence, fortitude, extraordinary courage, and commitment to this nation brought about radical change that was both effective and humane for the interrogation and debriefing of the prisoners at Abu Ghraib. Amazing! Likewise, Carol experienced heartbreak and misfortune in her personal life that would warrant giving up or settling for less given the circumstances of one's life. But not Carol. She rose above her pain with a spirit of triumph, holding tight to her commitment to faith, family, and the purpose of her mission. When duty called, Carol stepped up. She demonstrated characteristics of strength, adaptability, hard work, creativity, perseverance, and love for mankind that are an inspiration to us all.

Well done, Colonel Rogers! We are forever grateful and thankful for your service.

> **Dr. Pamela Paul, Licensed Psychotherapist &**
> **Christian Counselor, Largo, Florida**

When DUTY Calls

Raising My Family While Serving My Country

Colonel Carol Rogers

atmosphere press

I dedicate this book to my children,
Kelly, Amy, Bobby, Joe, and Frank,
who lived in my story

Table of Contents

Prologue

I was alone in my hooch at Abu Ghraib, Iraq. I looked around, devastated. I was overwhelmed with a sense of despair. I burnt a piece of sage (given to me by a friend) to rid the space of darkness and any evil lurking there. As the smoke spread throughout the room, I cried and prayed, sobbing and desperately pleading, "Oh God, this is worse than I imagined it would be. This is too much; it is more than I can handle. I can't do this. I am way over my head." What was a mother of five doing here in a combat zone? How did I get here? Why was I here? Is this how an Army Colonel, just sent to command the Joint Interrogation and Debriefing Center at Abu Ghraib should be feeling?

1

Dad: A Hero's Influence

I did not grow up wanting to be a soldier. However, I was so proud of my father's service in World War II (WWII). This Army seed was planted back in grade school. Every year for "Show and Tell" I would take my father's Silver Star and its corresponding citation to school and read:

> "For gallantry in action on 2 February 1944 in the vicinity of Cairo, Italy. Volunteering to guide his company platoons into position through an area swept by deadly machine gun fire which had already inflicted numerous casualties among his comrades, Private First Class Hemmerling wisely chose the least exposed route and began leading the platoons to their objective. When the enemy opened up with a second machine gun and delivered withering crossfire, he continued, calmly and courageously, to lead the men through the inferno of small arms fire and bursting shells. Unfaltering in the performance of duty, Private First Class Hemmerling successfully guided all four platoons into their new positions by moving speedily and aggressively and retaining his calmness under the most harrowing conditions, he allowed the units ample time for fortifying

their positions against a forthcoming enemy counter-attack. His gallant action reflects great credit upon himself and the Armed Forces of the United States."

I was close to my dad, but I wasn't the little girl standing on her father's shoes as they danced together. I was his only daughter and my father didn't know what to do with a girl. My father never talked to me about his experiences in the Army, but years later I had a son, Bobby, who adored his grandfather and grew extremely close to him. My father shared the story behind his Silver Star and citation with Bobby. It was Italy, 1944. My father's unit was on a hill, surrounded by Germans. The unit was struggling to maintain their position. They had lost some leaders and many members of the unit, and supplies were getting low. The word was circulating throughout the camp, they were out of options and the unit was going to surrender the next day. My father was of German heritage and his full name was Albert Adolf Hemmerling. This German name, middle name Adolf as in Hitler, was the name engraved on his dog tags. When my father heard the rumors of surrendering, he rationalized, "If I get caught, I will be regarded as a traitor, not a 'prisoner of war,'" so he decided he was leaving; he was NOT going to surrender. He went through the unit, asking everyone for any extra ammunition or weapons, because as he told his fellow soldiers, "You won't need them—you are going to surrender." He waited until the dark of night and carefully descended the hill, through dense enemy territory. However, when he turned around, the whole unit was following him. He ultimately led most of his unit to safety, earning for himself the Silver Star.

In my mind, my father was a giant. He was 5 feet, 8 inches. He was a humble man, accepting of people and truly authentic—he would look at someone and reason to himself, "I've got your number, but I am going to accept you anyway." He started as a Private (E-2) and eventually rose to the rank of Staff Sergeant (E-6). He was not a trained leader when he earned his Silver Star. He was a Private First Class (PFC), one grade from the lowest enlisted man in the Army. The two-star general who signed the award had to be wondering where his officers and senior enlisted soldiers were and why this PFC was leading the platoon. As brave as this action was, it took a long time for my father to talk about it, and when he did, he minimized his role. This was my father, a quiet and humble hero. This is my heritage and also my brothers' and our children's. My brothers and I learned determination from him, and maybe bullheadedness, as well. I believe both served us well.

My father risked his life in this thing called "war" and came home a hero. He was not publicly acclaimed, but my mother was proud of him, and my teachers all seemed impressed when I shared his gallantry. All I knew about war was people fought and died for their country, and this was an honorable thing to do. So, as a grade school student in the post-WWII, mid to late 1950s, when we had air raid drills at school and people saw Communism as a viable threat to our country, I saw defending my country as a noble profession. Those were the social norms and the dedication to country surrounding me and watering the seed which would grow into my own Army career

I was raised in the blue-collar city of Buffalo, New York, the oldest child and only daughter of Marge and Al, along with three younger brothers, Butch, Allan, and David, who were one, two, and five years younger than me respectively. I was part of the baby boomer generation resulting from men returning from WWII, getting married, and having kids. My father enlisted in June 1942, months after the bombing of Pearl Harbor and the US entry into WWII. He returned home when the war was over in 1945 and married my mom one year later. I was born in 1947.

Despite my father having to drop out of school in the

eighth grade to help support the family when his father died, he was the smartest man I ever met. He could fix ANYTHING. Consequently, we didn't throw anything broken away because my dad was going to fix it. It also didn't matter if he had the right tools: he could fix a muffler by attaching a used frozen orange juice can around the hole, or the waffle iron by replacing the worn-out cord with a cord from another appliance. He worked at Westinghouse as a machine repairman, and he had an innate sense of how machines worked.

My parents were lower class and worked their way to working middle class. When I was seven, my father built us a new home. My brothers shared one large bedroom, and I had my own room. My parents planted a lilac tree outside my bedroom window, and to this day, whenever I smell lilacs, it takes me back to living in our home. My father did whatever work he could on the house himself, by working well into the night after work and all day on the weekends. He would take whatever money was left from his weekly pay, after paying the bills and buy whatever building supplies he needed for the next week. He lived in that house until he died at 84, along with my mom who died a few years after. My father built our house, and it was a grand house—a brick front, a living room with a fireplace, a separate dining room and a full basement, which he eventually finished off as well. We had a sprawling lawn in front and a large backyard bordering a wooded area. In the back was the clothesline where we hung our clothes to dry. We were so proud of that house, and oh, the memories we collected there over the years.

My mother had a mental image of what an ideal mother-daughter relationship should look like, dreaming of being best friends, telling each other everything, and enjoying doing everything together. I was not that daughter. My mother lost her own mother when she was only two years old, and she lived with an aunt until she was seven, when her father remarried. Her aunt used to tell her, "Stepmothers are mean and punish you for nothing. They put you in closets and make you sit there by yourself." Did these stories sabotage a potentially good relationship between my mom and her new stepmother? Despite her tumultuous childhood, my mom was a go-getter. She had a high school diploma and worked nights at the telephone company when we were little, so she could be home to take care of my brothers and me during the day. She was devoted to all her children, but she had a wicked temper and practiced corporal punishment, which was commonly accepted during the '50s and '60s when we were growing up. My brothers received the wooden spoon across their butts more than I did. I learned early to be a good girl, follow the rules, and do my share of the chores. As a child, I tried to make my mom happy. As I got older, I learned I didn't have this power, and I merely tolerated her. In my teenage years, my mom and I were constantly crashing. I disliked her on one hand, but I carried a deep love for her on the other. I never took time to listen to and accept my mother as she was. If I had tried, if I was different, maybe she would have been different.

When I was in sixth grade, something happened that changed my trajectory in life. Our parish opened a Catholic school, and my parents transferred my brothers and me from the local public school. I was resistant to the new school and did not want to leave my friends, but it was the best decision my parents could have made. In fifth grade, I had become friends with a girl who, even at the age of ten, was a free spirit. I remember Linda—a red-haired little wild cat. (Later, as an adult, she did stand-up comedy and had a great Phyllis Diller routine.) I was attracted to the unruliness of her life; we were always off on an adventure. We would sneak into her uncle's room when he was at work. Linda would open his dresser drawer, pull out this deck of pornographic playing cards, and show me the nude men and women—I was fascinated by them, knowing it was not something we should be looking at. At Girl Scout meetings after school, we would lock the doors to the stalls in the restrooms, crawl underneath, and leave. We were so mischievous we were both required to leave our Girl Scout troop. I don't remember being sorry about it—Linda and I were still a team, and we left together. We were 10 years old and already marked as "troublemakers." As the good little girl who always followed the rules, I was intrigued by the thrill of being naughty.

The next year, I found myself in a Catholic school and my teacher was Sister Miriam Xavier. Sister Xavier did not beat our knuckles with a ruler. Instead, she was sweet and loving. She would talk to us during the day, as if she enjoyed being with us. She and her dedication to Christ enthralled me. So, I decided on a vocation; I (like most of the girls in my class) was being called to become a sister of Mercy, like Sister Xavier. That did not last. However, what did stay with me for my whole life was a deep sense of faith. I was given beliefs and ideals I could aspire to, and I found a place I could go (both physically and metaphorically) for comfort and peace.

In sixth grade I had my first job. Someone gave my parents an old upright piano, and I took lessons. Around the time I started Catholic school, our parish priest, Father Doyle, needed an organist for the daily Latin Masses the Catholic Church celebrated. When he found out I played piano, he offered to pay for my organ lessons if I would become the organist for the daily Mass. Since I had never seen my father take a day off work, even if he was sick, I assumed the same sense of responsibility. I was at church for 7 a.m. Mass every day from 6th grade until 10th grade. Father Doyle was fast and prayed a Mass at 7, 7:30, and 8am On Saturdays there could be six or eight Masses, every half hour. Some mornings my mother would drive me, but otherwise I would walk the half-mile to the main road and take a bus. Either way, I was always there. I have an image in my mind of a stockpile of prayers from all those Masses I can tap into any time in my life when I need them.

Father Doyle was reminiscent of the Irish Catholic priests played by Bing Crosby in the old movies. If he saw kids hanging around after school, he would load his car and take them all for ice cream. When the local Catholic college had a basketball game, he would buy tickets and take the boys' basketball team. When the school put on a St. Patrick's Day program in his honor, he was so touched he immediately gave everyone the next day off, much to the chagrin of the sisters who ran the school. I had the same attitude toward work in high school when I started babysitting. I remember once missing a big party because I had already promised to babysit. A voice inside me told me I committed to babysit, and I had to follow through. I hated missing the party, but I did not see any options. My parents never talked about work ethic or a sense of integrity; they lived it, and I assumed this was how things were done.

Close to graduating, I was talking to my cousin about what she planned to do after high school. I joked, "Get married?" Marriage was the furthest thing from my mind. I was going to college to become a teacher. I remember her response because it shocked me: "Yeah, might as well; there's nothing better to do." One day after I had started college, my aunt was talking to my mom. She was worried that I was going to be an old maid; I had to be pushing 20. Looking back, this was a depiction of the world I was raised in, the expectations and goals (or lack of goals) for women.

Of about 15 cousins my age, only one older male cousin and I went to college. Neither of my parents or any of their siblings had furthered their education. Both my parents treated me as if I was the smart one of their children. It was not because I was a genius, which was far from the truth. I studied hard and got good grades. My brothers are all unquestionably intelligent as well, but they didn't receive the same message I did. In fact, talking to one brother recently, he told me Mom told him he was not "college material." So, he never applied himself in school. My mom suggested college as an option to me, and as a result I was the only child in our family to go on to college and get a degree. Living in Buffalo in the '60s, it seemed women had four choices: teacher, nurse, secretary, or beautician. There may have been more at the time, but no one I knew talked about them or exposed me to them. My mom, more so than my dad, saw getting a college degree as the height of education. The degree had to be functional (like teaching), but it wouldn't matter which college I earned it from. In my mind I decided merely getting a degree earned me a sense of respectability.

I would have been overwhelmed at a large university; so, although I applied and was accepted to the University of California, Los Angeles and the University of Buffalo, instead, I chose a small college, the State University of New York at Fredonia, and it was the best choice I could have made. Fredonia was perfect for me—a smaller university in a quaint little town with tree-lined streets and old, well-kept homes. We could walk to the local hangouts (mostly bars). The drinking age in New York was 18. We could walk to the movie theaters and a local playhouse. I loved it. At home, I worked summers as a waitress and throughout the school year I worked in the cafeteria for breakfast and lunch, to help cover my living expenses. Back in the late '60s, early '70s I could make enough in one summer to cover one semester of college, and I was also able to get a modest student loan for the money I needed to cover the deficit. I am shocked to see how tuition has skyrocketed since. It never occurred to me not to work—how else was I going to afford college?

Fredonia was far enough from home I had to board at school, but close enough I could come home for a weekend. The boys' and girls' dormitories were separate, and they were locked at curfew, which was 10 p.m. on weekdays and midnight for weekends. I loved everything about college: my classes, the social life, and living with a group of girls in the dormitory. I was exposed to personalities I had never met before, especially in my Catholic school community back home. At Fredonia, I met Jewish girls who were as devout as any Catholic girls I knew. I met girls who were having sex with their boyfriends. They were not in any way corrupted or without values. They didn't look trashy or any different from the other girls. I decided I liked them, and it didn't matter if they shared my religious beliefs or even my moral beliefs. They were good people. I was seeing life and people differently than I had in my little world in Buffalo. The world and possibilities were opening to me.

My first week at college, a "cool guy" took notice of me. I remember him being adorable, with white-blond hair and blue eyes. He was confident and a little cocky. Evidently, he did not get the memo that I was a "nice girl" but not worth dating. He was my first boyfriend, and I found there was something about me he liked. I was enjoyable and dating material. I was thrilled. I never dated or had a boyfriend in high school. The guys in our group of friends would come and talk to me about their girlfriends, but I was not anyone's girlfriend. I only dated this guy for a few months, but it didn't go very far, possibly because I carried with me the limitations on relating to boys I learned at Catholic school. We could kiss, but no more.

2

Love: Young and Foolish

I met Bob the summer before my junior year. We instantly started dating exclusively and after six months, unexpectedly, at Christmas he proposed. I wasn't ready, but I loved him and it seemed like a natural progression. We planned to get married in July and finish our final year of college as a married couple. Each relationship from my first boyfriend leading to Bob had more and more depth. My mom was furious when she found out Bob would only be 20 when we got married, thereby requiring a parent's signature. She told me, "He is too young to make such a commitment. You should wait a year." I was bullheaded. This was my mom trying to control my life, and we fought against it. Although my dad often let my mom have her way, Bob turned to my dad for his opinion. My father responded with his characteristic wisdom, "As long as you love my daughter and treat her well, I don't care if you are 15 or 50." All arguments ended and we continued with plans for a July wedding.

Second semester, junior year, Bob bought a mobile home, reasoning he could get a roommate for the semester and we would have a home after we got married. It was a great idea, except it also provided us a place where we could be alone. His roommate had a girlfriend in his hometown and went home most weekends to see her. So, there we were in this beautiful new mobile home, where we could watch TV on the couch to-gether, or lay on the bed for a nap together. As a good Catholic girl, with dreams of my virgin wedding night, I was too naive to see this was a recipe for disaster.

Bob supported my request to wait, and we were both lim-iting how far we went when we were making out. However, I vividly remember one night in February when I feared we had gone too far. I backed off from Bob and vowed to try harder to wait until the wedding. But in early March, I missed my period. Bob was skeptical, naively convinced I could not be pregnant. I made a doctor's appointment, and I remember the shame of the visit. It was my first female exam, and I was nervous and scared. The doctor was abrupt and cold. He gave me some pills to bring my period on within a week if I was not pregnant, but he said disgustedly, "Young lady, you are most likely pregnant. You brought this on yourself; you will have to deal with it." During the week, I spent most of my time in my dorm room in bed, except for going to classes and church. I prayed like I had never prayed before for help and for strength. I could not believe I let this happen. I was too ashamed to talk to anyone during the week, except Bob. My mom and grandmother unexpectedly came to visit, bringing a book of invitations for the wedding, hoping I could choose a pattern or style, so they could be printed. Not wanting to have the "pregnancy" conversation until I was sure, I feigned a flu and I looked haggard enough they believed me, and I told them I would come home the next weekend and choose an invitation.

I did, in fact, go home next weekend, but mainly to tell my parents I was pregnant. Bob came with me, but I told him I wanted to tell my mother privately. She was terribly upset, and my father seemed so disturbed with me. He looked at me with disgust. "How could you?" His words and the look he gave me stung like a slap in the face, but this was the consequence of getting pregnant; I disappointed people. They were even more distraught when I told them I wanted to get married the next week. I reasoned it was not about me anymore, but about this baby I was carrying. It was March. If we married now, she would be born eight months later, and it would be close enough to nine months. Critical comments would be limited. Looking back on the whole process now, I can't help but smile at my own naiveté. I was a young woman trying to make decisions based on stringent and unyielding morals, morals that would eventually change and shift over the course of time.

Despite my parents being upset and disappointed, they rallied together, and in one day, I planned my wedding. We arranged for Father Doyle to marry us, decided to have the wedding reception at my parents' house, and went shopping for my wedding dress. My mom made me call and invite my relatives. I called my Aunt Delores, my father's sister, knowing she would spread the word for me to the rest of the family. After talking a while, she couldn't help herself, and blurted out, "But why are you moving your wedding date from July to March?" I responded Bob and I couldn't wait, so we changed the date. Knowingly, she exclaimed, "Well, of course we'll be there; we'll all be there."

I called my best girlfriend to come shopping with us for my wedding dress. When we stopped by her house, I met her at the door, and while walking to the car, I quickly told her what was happening. I remember going shopping on that gray day in Buffalo, snow still on the ground. I was sitting in a car between my mother and best friend, who were both crying. My eyes were dry. I had made my decision, and I was at peace.

My mom took me to a store that recently had a fire. They were trying to salvage some of their inventory that had survived and were having a huge sale. There we found a simple white dress for my wedding. The dress was sooty with smoke damage. The symbolism was not lost on me: a tarnished dress for a tarnished girl.

Bob's parents were a welcome contrast to mine. I remember his mom's exact words, with fondness and gratitude:

"Such is the love of a woman; she doesn't always love wisely, but always too well."

We had a lovely little wedding the following Saturday. Father Doyle married my parents and baptized my brothers and me, and now was marrying us, and he ignored the established Lenten restrictions and provided flowers and music for the church ceremony. It turned into the small wedding I always wanted, held in the basement of our house, instead of the big reception hall my mom was planning for July. At the end of the evening, with the party still going, Bob and I changed our clothes and rushed out of the house to the airport, where we flew student standby to New York City for the weekend before returning to school to finish the semester. Not a class act, but I remember it fondly and don't regret at all not having a larger wedding and more elaborate honeymoon in July.

I started the fall semester of my senior year, attending classes every day until Sunday, November 3, 1968, when Kelly was born. Seeing this beautiful baby, born of innocent love, dismissed any shame I had been carrying. My mom, who refused to come to my baby shower because "I didn't deserve one," was immediately the biggest fan of this new child. My whole family went from condemning me to being there to welcome the new arrival. All was right in the world.

I was back in class a week later, rushing home between classes to nurse. We were adjusting to our new life of balancing the demands of school and having a baby. I remember our first Christmas. We chopped a Charlie Brown Christmas tree from my uncle's field, bought one package of bulbs and one string of lights, and spent hours stringing popcorn to decorate the tree. It was the most beautiful tree in the world. We were a happy family and enjoyed the holidays with our extended families. This was the beginning of almost 40 years of Christmas Eves at my parents' house. And as our families grew, the parties grew. To this day, the kids and I remember fondly those Christmas Eves, with my brothers and their kids and eventually their grandkids, and anyone else my parents extended their open invitation to.

However, in January 1969 at the end of my first semester, I became horribly ill with the "Hong Kong" flu. When I went to the doctor, I found out I was also pregnant again. I was too sick to take my exams and start the final semester of my senior year. Bob also dropped out of school and looked for a job. Our best-laid plans seemed to be falling apart. We finally sold our mobile home and rented a small apartment back in Buffalo, where Bob took a job as an insurance salesman. I spent my time making curtains and reupholstering secondhand furniture and making our little apartment a home. However, in June, when I should have been with all my classmates who were graduating, I had a huge twinge of disappointment. I immediately dismissed it. It was another consequence I had to live with.

In October, as my delivery date came closer, I reasoned I would have to deliver by Thursday to be home in time to celebrate Kelly's first birthday on Monday. The growing baby inside, Amy, was on board with this and sure enough, in the wee hours of the morning on October 30, 1969, our second blessing entered our lives. We came home from the hospital and had the family over for a welcoming to our second child, Amy, and a celebration of Kelly's first birthday.

Bob and I were having a difficult time financially; we had student loans and now two children to care for. I remember we had no money for Christmas gifts. We talked about it and the only viable solution was to hock my engagement ring. It seemed a small enough sacrifice, and we had the money to buy gifts for our girls as well as small gifts for our extended families. After Christmas, when Amy was a couple months old, I took a job processing a bank's daily transactions on a computer. These early computers were huge machines, recently introduced to businesses. I worked from 7 p.m. until the work was done, usually between 2 and 4 a.m. I would come home, get a little sleep before the girls woke, and take care of them during the day, same as my mother had done. I was able to save enough to take the four remaining classes at summer school and schedule my student teaching for the fall and get my degree by January 1971. I stuck by my plan, even when I found out early in the summer I was again pregnant. This time I had more "Are you out of your mind?" looks than excitement over a new child. But I plugged on with my classes and started student teaching in September. There was a state rule that if a teacher was pregnant, she could not teach beyond her sixth month, but I wasn't showing when I started, so no one questioned me. I finished my student teaching in early January and had enough credits to graduate. I elected to wait and attend the ceremony in June. On February 4, 1971, Bobby joined our family, within weeks after finishing my student teaching. Our first boy. I found it was easier having the third child than the second. By now, the girls had each other to play with, so their demands on me were reduced. And they were both intrigued by this new little creature I brought home.

While I was in the hospital, Bob had moved us into an apartment back in Fredonia so he could return to school for his degree. I wasn't sure we could afford it, but I wanted to support him, and it was his turn to finish his education. He was working part-time at school, and we were living on his student loans. The stress of having so much responsibility so young started to weigh on Bob. Perhaps my mom was right about the age thing. In the summer he came to me and said, "I love you. I love the kids. I need to get my head together if I am going to be a good husband and father." In some way, it made sense to me, so I supported his decision to "go figure things out." During the next few months, I did not know where he was. I had an infant and two toddlers, and no money. My car broke. Because I had no money to fix it, it was towed to a lot, and they started charging me parking fees. So, I sold the car, a 1954 Mercedes Benz, for a ridiculously low amount. But

I at least had grocery money. I remember being angry with Bob for abandoning us, but I defended him to my family when they started to criticize him. I was so conflicted. I finally had to move out of the apartment as I could not pay rent, and I moved back in with my parents. I found it difficult to develop a long-range plan when I was simply trying to feed my family. Amid this turmoil, Bob returned. He had not "got his head together" as he intended, but knew he loved us and wanted to be with us.

In June, my parents, Bob, and my three children all accompanied me to my graduation ceremony in Fredonia to receive my B.A. degree in Secondary Education English. I was proud of my accomplishment as I stood there two years after my original graduation date, with a husband and three children. Looking back now, I had the same persistence and commitment my father had, which he demonstrated in the building of our home. I might have looked like my mom (at least that's what people would tell me), but I also had traits I learned from my father.

One step forward, two steps back. That's how it seemed my life was going. I now had my degree, as well as three children. Bob had dropped out of school but was not working. We were living with my parents. It was difficult living at home, amidst the "I told you so's," but it was most difficult for Bob, who had to endure my mother finding something new wrong with him every day. But we humbly accepted the needed help. I volunteered to teach religious education to high school kids in my parish and I was putting my degree to good use. At the same time, Bob passed the exam and was offered a job in the Washington, DC Police Force. We were elated. He went ahead with his training and found us an apartment. Early in 1972, Kelly, Amy, Bobby (who were three, two, and one year old respectively) and I moved to our new home in Maryland, outside of DC. I took my new degree and applied at the local high school, which was adjacent to our apartment complex, and started substitute teaching.

Bob was smart and personable. He graduated from the Police Academy at the top of his class, winning a year of college at American University, so he could get his degree by going to school at night. He also had his choice of assignments and chose to work in the Georgetown area of DC. At the time, women were burning their bras and young coeds were happily bouncing all around Georgetown. I am not sure this was a factor, but Bob came home one night and shared, "I love you. I love the kids. I am not so sure I want to be married." He went off again to find himself, this time staying with a co-worker and making weekly visits to the children and me.

Maybe I was crazy, but I did not want him to come back because he saw me as some weak basket-case, falling apart, who could not make it without him. I wanted him to return simply because he loved me and wanted to be with me. So, every time he visited, I made sure I had a good meal on the table, the house was clean, the kids looked good, and I looked great. He again returned after a couple months. Every time he left and returned, it was a honeymoon period, and I had the illusion all was right with our marriage.

We went on for another year or so. Again, he came to me, but this time he blurted out, "I love the kids. . ." Maybe he was in yet another phase. But as he pulled away, distancing himself from me, I slowly accepted he was no longer in love with me. After this realization hit me, I packed the kids and we moved back to Buffalo with my mom. During this time, I was listless and aimless. I was grieving. How could we end it now? I decided it was not what I wanted, so I called him and bravely stated, "I want to come and see you." He paused and admitted, "I'm not sure I want to see you without the kids." I answered, "I'm coming anyway."

I flew to DC and when Bob met me at the airport, we got a hotel room instead of going home. As we sat in a sparse hotel room, with nothing but a bed and a dresser, he talked.

During the time we were separated, he looked back over our relationship and started to build a case against me. He complained, "You are always too tired to make love. Your whole life seems to be wrapped around the kids. We don't seem to have any fun anymore." He was right. I was tired all the time. I had three children under the age of five and I was maintaining the household, managing our finances, and substituting a few times a week. I wasn't any fun. But I never revealed any of this, perhaps starting a conversation about how to make our situation work. I bit my tongue, agreed with him, and made love once more. I didn't say, "I have dinner waiting for you every night and the kids get hungry and the meat gets overcooked while waiting. You socialize with people all day long and when you come home, you are too tired to connect with me, talk to me. I would love it if you helped with the kids, so I had the energy to have sex when we go to bed. I would like to have some fun as well." I'm not sure I even acknowledged this to myself. The only way I could get him to love me was to make life easy for him, keep quiet, and make love. So that's what I did. It was my role and my obligation. I am not sure where I got the idea from; my parents always supported and helped each other. All weekend long, whenever he talked about his needs, I simply agreed and made love again. I know now it was not solely his fault. My needs were not important to me. I could not identify them, much less express them. It was not until more recently in life I learned that by withholding who I am, I am doing my part to create a disconnect and distance in a relationship. And I am not being authentic and real. I was not being true to myself.

Shortly after our weekend together, Bob called and wanted me to come back home. Again, it was another honeymoon period. One thing changed; Bob wanted to manage our finances. He was the one with a full-time job. It made sense. When I was managing finances, I would pay our bills and whatever was left over had to cover groceries, gas, and our living expenses.

Bob managed things differently—I calculated a number I needed for the week for groceries and incidentals. He gave me that amount and put aside his gas and living expenses. He paid the bills with the remainder. I did not complain about anything. If he was late for dinner, instead of waiting for him, while I became more and more angry, the kids and I would eat and I would put a plate aside for him. If he didn't want to go somewhere with me, I would pack the kids and we would go by ourselves. It must have worked because years later, he recalled those being the best times of our marriage for him. They were not the best years for me. At first, if I blinked too long, I feared missing a cue and blowing everything. But after a while, this new way of being became easy, and I fell into the rhythm of this new attitude. I filled my life with other things. I was still substitute teaching, and I started teaching religious education at my church. I would go out to the movies or go shopping with my girlfriends. One night, after shopping, a friend suggested we should stop for a drink on the way home. I was expecting a cup of tea; she wanted an adult beverage, and she suggested this little bar. This seemed harmless enough. But the bar had music, and men started asking us to dance. I was shocked when she agreed. In my world, married women did not dance with other men when they were out alone. But she was having so much fun, so eventually I accepted an invitation to dance. This evening out started to become a regular event. It seemed harmless enough; I loved Bob. He was smart and charming and nobody I met ever compared to him in my eyes. I never hid the fact I was going out and I would often talk to him about the people I met. However, I unexpectedly met a man who was so like Bob, but older and more accomplished. He and Bob liked the same author, and their taste in music and their philosophies of life were the same. Plus, he appreciated me. He saw me as smart, funny, and attractive. I started seeing more and more of him.

During this time, Bob was becoming an alcoholic. I did not

know how to recognize an alcoholic. I saw my father drinking, but I never saw him drunk. For me, the first indication someone was drunk was they couldn't walk, or they fell over. I never saw this, so I assumed Bob's drinking was normal. When he told me how stressful being a DC police officer was and it helped him to have a beer with his co-workers on the way home to take the edge off his day, I accepted it. I did not know at the time the beer was a six-pack, or more, and not always with his police friends.

One night, I came home from a date with this other man and Bob was already home. He had been caught and charged with drinking on duty and risked losing his job. I told him where I was. It was a difficult night for both of us. I hadn't previously lied to Bob, but I hadn't been forthcoming, either. I leveled with him and told him about my other relationship. He had always trusted me, and that trust had been abused. I had never been physically intimate with this other man—when I spoke my marriage vows to Bob, I promised fidelity. If I couldn't honor my promise to a man I loved, how could my word be any good to anyone? However, even though I did not betray Bob physically, I was emotionally unfaithful—I was giving emotions belonging to my husband to another man. After we talked, I re-focused. My primary obligation was to work this out with Bob. I never saw the other man again. However, everything I had been holding in, all those unspoken needs, now came out. Bob and I never argued, but we started fighting all the time. Perhaps, if we had looked for some professional help, we could have worked things out. But we didn't and finally I wanted him to leave. I hoped the same thing would happen to me that happened to him three times before. I hoped I would fall in love with him all over again. It never happened. We were classic examples of marrying and having children too young. Neither of us was prepared for the responsibility and maturity marriage requires, and by the mid '70s we separated.

Strangely, my good Catholic upbringing did not instill in me the dedication to my marriage, causing me to stay and work harder on it. Both Bob and I naively saw the struggles our parents had while we were adolescents as something inherently wrong with marriage. I remember talking before we were married, and we consciously agreed if we got to the point we did not love each other, we would separate rather than expose our children to a loveless marriage. Later in life, I walked in on my parents, in their 70s, sitting on the couch, holding hands, and watching television, and I got it. I told my mom, "I wish I had known when I was much younger that if I hung in there, was patient and committed to my relationship, this is what I could have."

This was a difficult time for the kids as well. When Bob called to say he was coming to visit, they would watch out the bedroom window for him to come around the corner, sometimes never coming. I am not sure if it was the drinking or his new life that caused him to miss many of these visits. My heart would ache for the kids. I was angrier with Bob about how he treated the kids than I was for anything he did to me while we were married.

He finally went back to work for the Police Department, but in a new undercover job. We were each separately managing our finances. Bob's method of financing did not work, and soon we were terribly in debt. I was out of cycle for a full-time teaching position, so I took the first job I could find in the accounting office of the University of Maryland. Bill collectors would call me and demand payment, because when they called for Bob at the Police Department, the Department would not acknowledge Bob's employment due to his undercover status. Since my name was on all the credit cards and bills, I contacted each debtor and made arrangements to send a lesser amount, but I would send it regularly. However, there still wasn't enough money to support my family. Money was tight.

I can remember washing our clothes in the bathtub, because I didn't have money for a laundromat. I was struggling to make ends meet. I was the hamster running around the wheel in his cage and getting nowhere.

3

Initiation: A Single Mom in the Army

What does a woman do when she finds herself 28 years old, separated from her husband, caring for three small children, working a menial job, and struggling to keep her head financially above water with no other prospects in sight? She joins the Army. But this was NOT the answer that immediately came to mind back in 1975

I had a friend, Madeleine, who was an officer in the Army Reserves. She suggested I consider joining. She explained the Army Reserves was a good part-time job; I could meet some new people, have some interesting assignments, and use the education degree I earned in college if I came in as an instructor. Even though I was so impressed with my father's military experience, it never occurred to me to personally consider the Army as a career. One day, while on the phone with my mother, she commented that she had recently read an article stating women were joining the military as a fulfilling career. Since she didn't laugh me off, I started to seriously consider the possibility. The idea intrigued me, and the anticipated discipline was something familiar to me. However, as a young mother, I did not fit the image I had in my mind of a soldier. Wasn't the Army for guys, not girly-girls like me? I was not an athlete; I did not consider myself tough. I loved being a girl—what could I possibly do in the Army?

I would often hang out with my brothers, who were all close in age to me, and their friends. I was the oldest, so of course I could do anything they could do. Venture into an abandoned house and crawl out onto the roof? Of course. Crawl into the narrow holes in the old bear caves at Allegheny State Park? No problem. But as I followed them on all these adventures, I was often terrified. But I would never say so. Maybe I wasn't so girly. So, I took the necessary tests and got the required physical. The next thing I knew, at 28 years old and a single parent to Kelly, Amy, and Bobby (6, 5, and 4 years old respectively) on July 12, 1975, I raised my hand before the US Flag, took my oath, and enlisted in the 1st' Women's Army Corps (WAC) Basic Training Battalion, 80th Division (Training). I received a uniform and started attending drills. I took an assignment as an instructor and entered the military as a Private First Class, and upon completion of Basic Training, I was promoted to Specialist 4. Little did I know at the time the powerful impact the oath of allegiance to my country would have on my life.

Because of my trepidation about being too "girly" for the Army, I braced myself for basic training. I was sent to Ft. Mc-Clellan, Alabama—the same place my father attended basic training some 35 years earlier. I fear the small prop airplane that took me from the Atlanta airport to Ft. McClellan was the same antiquated aircraft my father rode years ago. As I sat in the rickety plane, bouncing all over, I grasped my seat. Would we make it? I was not the normal picture of a recruit going off to basic training. I was 5 foot 2 inches, weighed about 100 pounds soaking wet, and I had three kids.

One of the requirements for enlistment as a parent was to sign a statement acknowledging my responsibilities as a mother would not be accepted as an excuse to avoid mobilization. The statement read that I would be expected "to be available for mobilization, if required, and to accept such assignments as are in the best interest of the service, regardless of my marital status and/or responsibility for dependents. I further accept my responsibility to make appropriate arrangements for the care of my dependents in the aforementioned circumstances and if I am required to perform duty in an area where dependents are not authorized." In compiling my Dependent Care Plan, my parents were designated the people responsible for my children if I had to leave. This document became part of my file the Army maintained. The Vietnam War was over. There was nothing brewing in the world hinting at possible deployment. So, I presented this request to my parents as a mere formality. I might have to answer the call if a situation arose threatening the United States. But I did not dwell on it; there was no sense worrying about something that hadn't happened yet. I was secure in the knowledge that if it happened, my children would be with people they knew and loved, and I needn't worry. When I went to Basic Training, my parents came and took Kelly, Amy, and Bobby to their house. They were still working, and my grandmother watched them during the day. My family extended themselves for me. I did not acknowledge it at the time. I was involved and centered on my own life and didn't have the wherewithal to consider other people and what was going on in their lives. But I relied on them, and they were always there.

I've learned everything in life is a matter of perspective. At home I worked a full-time job, maintained a household, and cared for my three children by myself. When I arrived at Basic Training and my drill sergeant told me I had to make my bed and help clean the latrine in the morning, I was stunned. That was it? Did she know I was used to waking in the morning, getting three kids fed, dressed and off to daycare or school, deciding what to have for dinner and if I would have to stop at the store, make the beds, clean the breakfast dishes, wash and dress myself, and head off to work for the day? And she told me for the next couple weeks the Army would do my thinking for me. I didn't have to decide what to have for dinner or if I needed to grocery shop. This was not difficult. It was a cake-walk compared to my civilian life. This perspective worked to my advantage as I compared my life in basic training to my busy life back home. Consequently, the drills of basic training did not frustrate or challenge me as much as they did my younger, single, childless counterparts.

Basic Training pushed me more physically than mentally. I was never a "jock" in school. Yes, I was on the girls' softball and basketball teams, but I was one of the players the coach put in when we had a lead in the score and they wanted to make us poorer players feel part of the team. So, to be starting my day with pushups and a run was a new phenomenon for me. But the drill sergeants added "jodies" (marching songs) to our runs, and I surprisingly got into it: "Mama, Mama, don't you see, what the army's doing to me? Took away my loving man. Now I sleep with Uncle Sam." There was another one I enjoyed, "One mile, no sweat. Two miles, better yet. Three miles, looking good. Four miles—Hollywood." This made running so much fun. Later, I remember teaching these jodies to my kids and sometimes slipped from mother to drill sergeant when they begrudgingly came running with me. Basic training taught me the fundamentals of being a soldier. Not only did we have physical training, but we also learned military customs and courtesies: who and when to salute; how to properly wear our uniform, how to march in formation. We learned the legal aspects of military law, what we were accountable for as soldiers, and how we treated enemy soldiers in the event of a conflict. We learned how to fight—how to fire various weapons, military tactics, and strategies. It was impressed on us this information could save our lives someday.

After basic training, I settled into life in the reserves. I was living in Beltsville, Maryland at the time, working full time at the University of Maryland, and attending reserve drills one weekend a month. It was a grueling schedule, especially for a single mom. Reservists are required to attend 12 monthly drills and two weeks of Annual Training (AT) every year. You earned points for each, and this added to a qualifying year for retirement purposes in the reserves. I enjoyed my weekend drills and annual training. I loved the structure and the sense of purpose it gave me. I was at home in the Army. Maybe an Army career wasn't so outlandish.

The children were having their own adjustments to life without their father. Bobby was having an especially difficult time. He was four years old, the age when a little boy starts looking for his male identity, and there was no one around. He was so angry all the time. If he stubbed his toe, he was mad at the world. I talked to Bob, who as an undercover cop was running a Floral Shop in Georgetown. I suggested maybe Bobby could live with him until summer, when the girls were out of school. He agreed. On Saturdays, Bobby would come and stay with the girls and me, and on Sundays the kids would all go and stay with Bob. This worked well and the kids could have time with each other as well as each of their parents. I could immediately see the difference in Bobby. Maybe he would like to stay with his father through the summer? But he decided, "No, when the girls are done with school, I'm coming home again." It was almost as if he knew he needed this time, but when it was over, he wanted to come home.

At some point, Bob left the Police Department and moved to Iowa, and the child support he was giving me stopped. Even with the extra income I was earning as a member of the Army Reserves, I was having trouble managing the financial and logistical responsibilities of a single mom. In the summer, the kids went to Buffalo to spend time with my family, so I got another part-time job, working as a waitress in the evening for the dinner hours. Although this put a dent in my bills, I worried about bringing my children back to the apartment complex we lived in. There were some robberies, and a reported rape. Yet, I couldn't afford to upgrade. I was so conflicted. I loved the reserve unit I was attached to; I enjoyed the people at the University of Maryland I worked with. I liked having my own place, and I was dating a nice man at the time. I, selfishly, did not want to leave all of this and move back to Buffalo and start over.

To aggravate an already dismal situation, my mom was continually pressuring me to come home. There were no good options. As much as I hated to do it, at the end of summer 1976, I packed my things and moved from the DC area back to Buffalo, NY. I was now without a job or a place to live. I again moved in with my parents. I was angry about the turn my life had taken and (as selfish as it was) my mother became the focus of my anger. I was not an easy person to live with. I earnestly started looking for work. I enrolled the kids in the local school, and it was a much better school system than the one they left. Bobby was starting kindergarten and Kelly and Amy were in third and second grade respectively. The kids loved being back in Buffalo and having extended family around; in addition to their grandparents, there were aunts, uncles, and lots of cousins, all around their age.

A month after moving back to Buffalo, I was fortunate enough to be hired for a program at Erie County Central Police Services. Within the first few days, my superiors singled me out from our group of 20 hires to be the manager of the group. I also found an apartment around the corner from my parents. Finally, I joined the 98th Training Division in Buffalo, as an instructor in a supply/food service-training unit. I still worked full time and attended monthly drills and annual training. It made a world of difference having friends and family around as a support system. Additionally, the cost of living in Buffalo was much less than the DC area, and I was able to relax and manage our life a little better.

We had a three-bedroom upstairs apartment, furnished with the things we had brought from Maryland. We lived in a neighborhood with plenty of other kids for my children to play with, whose mothers were all around my age, and we formed a tight group. My kids attended a good school, and my parents were right around the corner. However, I still wasn't satisfied. I started doing some soul-searching, trying to decide what direction I wanted to go in next. I didn't know what I wanted to do with my life. I saw my job at Erie County Central Police Services as temporary; there wasn't much upward mobility there. I needed to find a profession allowing me to support my family better and use the education and talents I had. I learned through my teaching experience in Beltsville, MD that teaching high school English was not what I wanted to do with my life. But I was at a loss as to what else I could do with an education degree. I sought some vocational counseling and, after a series of tests, the professions I scored highest on were Army officer and lawyer. I knew I didn't have enough money for law school, but I found I could get a second degree as a paralegal, so I enrolled and started night school. I loved the legal courses—researching, building a case, and finding and citing other cases with similar issues. I was working days and going to school four nights a week and studying in between. I loved my courses, and the homework seemed so relevant it was almost fun. I could not wait to graduate and go to work at a law firm. I was moving in the right direction, getting an education leading me to a new career.

The children seemed to be doing well, also. I would come home, grab a quick dinner with them, and drop them off at my parent's house while I went to school. I would return in time to get them, take them home, and put them to bed. I would study in the evenings and during my work lunch hours, but I tried to save time for the kids on the weekend. When I went to get my kids, they were often playing Monopoly or other games with my mom. She was good at taking time to play with the kids. They loved SCAT, a card game. She would give them pennies out of her coin bank to play with, and she let them keep what they won, turning them into little gamblers scoring 50 to 75 cents on a good evening.

The children had friends in the neighborhood and school, and their cousins were often at my parents' when they were there. There were always plenty of other kids to invite to their birthday parties. Bobby, whose birthday was in February, had tobogganing parties at Chestnut Ridge, a local park providing summer and winter activities. Both the girls' birthdays were around Halloween, so one year they had a slumber Halloween birthday party in the country at my father's hunting cabin, which was an old and creaky farmhouse. At night, you could hear mice and other critters running around the attic. I went earlier and "haunted" the house. I turned off the electricity, so we had to use candles. I put "spider webs" around as decorations along with hanging bats and stuffed black cats. I loaded all the girls into my father's truck and headed to the lodge. As the girls tiptoed in, the squeals and shrieks started. Bats and cats greeted them. On the stairway going to the bedrooms, they screamed at a life-sized goblin. When they were finally ready for bed, I took the clothes off the goblin and put them on myself. I walked over and stood in the doorway of the bedroom. As soon as they saw me, they started to scream. When they finally saw it was me, we fell over each other laughing. We all had a great closing to our Halloween eve

When I enlisted in 1975, women in the Army had their own corps—the Women's Army Corps (WAC). Around the time I moved back to Buffalo, the Army eliminated the WAC, and we were absorbed into the regular Army. My first unit in DC was a predominately female WAC unit, but this was not the case in Buffalo. Life in my new reserve unit was different from my old unit. Even though much of my unit was male, I don't remember being singled out or treated differently as a female. I do remember coming home from drills and crying to my mom about my day. And she would repeatedly respond,

"Carol, you need to get a thicker skin." I was dealing with the difficulties and frustrations of working with a diverse group of people, rather than being harassed because I was a female. I was simply another soldier. Of course, there were always some non-commissioned officers (senior enlisted) who would get off on their authority and yell at me (or anyone else) to get something done. Some days I took this better than others.

The Army Reserves provided family social opportunities during the year to help build camaraderie. Our family favorite was the unit Christmas party, for the members of the unit and their families. The kids and I always went, and it was a welcome experience to meet the families of the other reservists and to be part of the Army family.

Since the vocational counselor also suggested a career as an Army officer, I decided to become an officer. My three-year enlistment contract was ending. I enjoyed my time in the Army Reserves, I had the education, and I wanted to have a more demanding job and to earn better compensation for my time. When I decided to apply for Officer Candidate School (OCS), I was surprised at how difficult it was to find anyone in the unit to help me or to talk me through the process. Even though I read the regulations, I still had so many questions. Finally, our Command Sergeant Major (CSM), who was also our full-time administrative person, decided to help me. I prepared the necessary paperwork and applications, gathered the required documents, and sent my packet off. The last stage of the process was to go to an oral interview by a board of Army Officers. My CSM again provided insights and helped me prepare for the board, drilling me on military history and preparing me for this grueling event. I was living in Buffalo at the time and the interview was in Rochester, about 60 miles away. By the time I got the kids off to school, I was late leaving, and my heavy foot got me in trouble. I was stopped by the police on the way there for speeding, which made me even later. I arrived frazzled and had lost my peace of mind and focus before a potentially life-changing event. I had to pull myself together and get through the interview. I prayed, stood up straight, adjusted my uniform, remembered the coaching my CSM gave me, and entered the room.

I walked in and looked at the officers sitting in dress uniform, shoes shined and medals sparkling, looking intimidating and ready to test me. I gave myself a pep talk. "Smile. You've got this." I stood in front of them and started answering their questions. Soon my initial nervousness diminished, and I relaxed. I had prepared for this, and it was time to show these people I was officer material. I was confident about the interview and went back to Buffalo to await results. Despite my stressors along the way, I was selected for Officer Candidate School (OCS), which would result in commissioning as an officer in the US Army. I was slowly recognizing the significance of the Army in my life. I began seeing it as a long-term relationship for me. Getting my commission was crucial to my continuance.

4

Leadership: Inherent Ability or Learned Trait?

Can you train someone to be a leader? The military believes so. They were sending me to school to learn how to be a leader. I had some natural leadership tendencies. I held offices in our church high school youth group. I started a sorority in freshman year. I developed and coordinated activities for our youth group, including dances drawing over 100 people. I even planned bike trips and outings continually for my friends and me. People seemed to go along with my ideas. But I never looked at this as leadership. In fact, I was nominated and lost the election for president of our youth group by one vote—mine. I saw my opponent as a better leader than me. At Central Police Services, I was selected over the other members of my group, including three men, to lead the group. So, I had some leadership qualities, but there was much more I had to learn about being a leader and accepting the role. Officer Candidate School (OCS) was the beginning of this training.

OCS was designed to train soldiers to be officers by teaching tactics and techniques of leadership. It prepares candidates for the challenges of being an officer, from leading others to acknowledging military values, culture, and law. It challenged me physically, mentally, academically, and emotionally. OCS was taught at Camp Smith, which is adjacent to the West Point Military Academy in a beautiful mountainous area of eastern New York. West Point is the Army's premier service academy for the young men and women who are selected based on rigorous criteria for enrollment, and it prepares them for "a career of professional excellence and service to the nation." The Senior West Point Cadets were our tactical (TAC) officers (or instructors) for our training. The Cadets were demanding and tough, but whatever task they required of us, they could perform five times better. I found them a humble lot. For example, some of my fellow students or Candidates, as we were called in OCS, were Vietnam veterans, which meant they served and survived one of the most controversial wars of the 20th century. They were men who believed in serving our country but decided if they were going to continue their service, it would be as an officer. One day a bright, young cadet commented to one of these veterans, "You have been to war. What can I possibly teach you? But I have my job to do, so I will continue as best I can." These brave young cadets graduated and were sent off to various assignments, many going on to serve their country as General Officers.

At OCS we learned leadership by holding leadership positions. We had mentors who watched us and provided feedback. One morning I was assigned as a Platoon Leader for the day. I had done a fairly good job, but at the end of the day I was pulled aside by a TAC officer, and he told me, "You are not going to make it. You are having trouble handling more than one task at a time." At first, I was shocked, followed by insulted, and finally indignantly astounded. It was a déjà vu moment, and I had a flashback, sitting quietly and listening to Bob tell me how I was not engaging in our marriage. I was not going to be silent this time. I looked at him. "You don't know anything about my life. I am a single mother of three, I work full time, and I maintain a household. I am carrying a full load at night school and going through OCS. I can handle more than one thing at a time." He was surprised and looked at me. Afterwards, I performed the same, but something changed. I was treated differently, and my leadership grades all improved. I expected people to automatically see me for who I was and what I could handle, without me pointing it out or proving it to them. However, I learned this is not the case. Sometimes I had to speak up for myself, or even point out the obvious. I hated confrontations, and I didn't like spotlighting myself, but there were times when both were necessary. I needed to believe in myself.

In addition to holding leadership positions, we also learned teamwork at OCS—we learned to depend on each other, whether navigating through the woods to determine where to meet with the rest of the unit or deciding how to get an injured member of our group over a raging river. This left an impression on me. I learned as a leader, I could not do it myself; I had to rely on others.

At OCS, there was a classmate I often clashed with. I'll call him Candidate Arrogant Bully. For whatever reason he seemed to dislike me. However, he seemed to wield control over others in this weekend OCS group. I was the only female in this weekend OCS training during the year. If I was talking to one of the guys in our group and Bully walked over, the guy talking to me acted embarrassed and quit talking or left. This happened with various people on different days.

One day for leadership training, Bully was the acting Commander, and I was his Executive Officer (the second in command). One of the acting Commander's duties was to call the group to attention and report to the instructor. Bully got called out at some point and tasked me to take over his responsibilities. Before class, we hung our jackets and milled around. At the designated time, I called the class to attention and was about to present the class to the instructor, when Bully came rushing in. He throws his jacket at me and tells me to hang it, while he jumps in to present the class to the instructor. I remember I grumbled something under my breath; I did not want to make a scene. It might have had something to do with him hanging his own damn jacket and letting me do the job he assigned me.

Later, after class, I met him in the hall, and we had a loud and heated conversation. I told him, "I did not appreciate your degrading attitude today at class; I was your Executive Officer, not your handy-maid."

Bully responded, "I was in charge, and you should have followed my orders. I was the senior officer."

I wasn't done with him. "I was following your orders. I was presenting the class to the instructor, until you burst in and threw your jacket at me."

He rebutted, "I was there on time, and it was my job to present the class."

We both had valid points, and I am not sure I would advise another soldier to handle it the way I did. Surprisingly, following this confrontation, Bully seemed to show me more respect; well, maybe not respect but deference. Afterwards, my TAC officer called me aside and wanted to know about our conversation. I told him we simply needed to clear the air, and he applauded me. "Good work, Rogers." In retrospect, maybe he was glad I handled it directly instead of going to him. It was the right approach. There was no need to get others involved. I learned from this experience, and over the years if I had an issue with someone, I tried to address it directly with the individual. Years later I ran into Bully when we both were captains. He acted as if I was his long-lost friend and recalled fond memories of our time in OCS together. He also told me he was getting out of the Army because he couldn't handle the "bullshit." Go figure.

OCS was much like basic training, testing us to see how we function under pressure, pushing us so we could see what we were made of. Everyone was challenged. But we learned from our mistakes. I remember early on in OCS, the cadets were always yelling, "What are the first three words out of your mouth?" to which we called out, "Sir, Candidate (Last Name)."

One day, this cadet came over and yelled, "What are the first three words out of your mouth?"

Try as I might, I could not remember "Candidate." I knew it had a "C" but my mind went blank, so I blurted out, "Sir, Commodore Rogers."

Well, even this disciplined, stern West Pointer could not keep a straight face, as he called over to his friends, saying, "Hey, guess what? We have a COMMODORE over here." I never did live this one down. But I never forgot my title again, and I learned our instructors had a sense of humor.

Finally, our tests were over, our leadership assessments were completed and the next day there was a commissioning ceremony for those of us who passed the training. It was the night before graduation and commissioning. I was going to meet with a couple other members of my class to decide what prank or trick we would play on the incoming class. This is a time-honored tradition in the military occurring at the completion of training, or when units are having various competitions (land navigation, physical training events, or exercises) where one unit is the blue team and the other the red team, with the goal of capturing a stronghold or other objective. This prank usually takes place after the completion of training or the event; the object is to find some clever, creative trick to play on the new class or competing unit. Over time, I have seen the Commander's car carried and placed on cinder blocks in the middle of the parade field, or the losing unit's guidon (unit flag) displayed in front of the winning unit's offices.

I planned to meet a couple OCS classmates on the parade field to discuss our options. While we were there, someone got the bright idea to get some beer to get the creative juices flowing. So, two of the guys went back to get the beer, and another went to get some snacks. I decided to wait for them in the guard shack on the parade field. Well, all of a sudden,

I see blue and red flashing lights and I hear a voice through a megaphone. "I'll go after this one. He went over the edge, into the ravine." I assumed it was the guy with the beer. Not wanting to get caught, I ducked into the closet and closed the door. Shortly thereafter, the Military Police (MP) entered to search the shack, and they opened the closet door and there I was, standing, looking extremely foolish. Imagine my embarrassment. They wanted my name, which unit I was assigned to, and what I was doing in the guard shack. I knew two things: I did not want them to know I was waiting for my friends to bring some beer and I did not want them to know I was scheduled to be commissioned the next day. So, I told them I was in the non-commissioned officer class, and I was waiting for my boyfriend. Yes, I lied. Not befitting of a soon-to-be officer in the US Army. Honesty is truly one of my cherished values. But I did not honor my word. I broke my own rule.

As the MPs were taking me back, we ran into my Commanding Officer (CO), who said, "I'll take her; she's one of mine," obviously blowing my cover. He proceeded to counsel me, asking, "What were you thinking?" and of course I had no rational answer. When we returned, my CO gathered my three partners-in-crime, who were worried about me. He sat us all for counseling, warning us we were all about to become officers and we had standards to maintain. He posed the question, "Carol, how did it look, you meeting three guys in the guard shack at night? I know all four of you and I know there was nothing going on, but you need to be aware of appearances." I did not consider this aspect; I was worried about getting caught with beer. But I would never be seen as "one of the guys" and I needed to be sensitive to this perception going forward in my career. This was an extremely valuable lesson to learn. In this case, my gender did make a difference.

After our counseling, we did take a few minutes to plan our prank on the incoming class. We waited for the class to fall asleep and I worked the female barracks, the guys worked the male barracks. We collected everyone's boots and put them in a huge pile on the parade field. The next morning, the women in my barracks started waking and dragging themselves to the showers. As they started dressing, I heard one new candidate say, "My boots are missing." Another one called out, "Where are my boots?" Soon the whole group was buzzing as they were scrambling, looking for boots. When it was finally discovered all the boots were in a pile on the parade field, there was mass mayhem. Everyone, male and female, was issued the same black boots. It was a monumental job, finding the right pair in a pile of about 200 boots, even for those who had put their name in their boots. I smiled gleefully to myself as I got dressed and prepared for my commissioning, my mischievous side showing again. I admit I was proud to be part of this ingenious plan.

Some might ask if I was harassed by men in the Army, Maybe. But it was to my advantage to not see it that way. Instead, I saw these situations as learning to deal with others in a professional environment. To be effective, I needed to learn to work with everyone. If I had interpreted attitudes toward me as harassment, I might have developed a "poor me" attitude and not have tried as hard. Or I might have become angry and put a chip on my shoulder. But instead, I directly dealt with a difficult situation.

My father taught my brothers and me that women were to be respected. Men don't hit women; men don't use their physical strength against women. I saw my parents as helpmates to each other, both working hard to support the family, especially in their productive years. Also, it would never occur to either of my parents that someone was picking on me simply because I was a girl. They knew me well enough to know if I got into skirmishes with my brothers, I could have as easily provoked it as my brothers. These attitudes formed how I looked at my interactions with men. This served me well as an officer in the military. I saw us all, both men and women, as soldiers. I only wanted to be a good soldier. I wanted to provide for my family. I did not see any barriers to this because of my gender.

5

Commissioned: A New Lieutenant's Challenges

On August 18, 1978, at 31 years old, I was commissioned a Second Lieutenant by the Empire State Military Academy. I was pleased my parents brought my kids to the ceremony, and they were part of the crowd, watching. Prior to the ceremony, I was in formation, waiting to march onto the parade field. They lined us by height and all five feet, two inches of me stood ready at the front of the line. I was full of anticipation to get my "butter bars" (gold bars of a second lieutenant). My kids saw me and started jumping up and down and waving—they were 7, 9, and 10 years old at the time. I remember smiling, so proud to be their mom. One of the cadets came over to me, "Are those your kids?" I looked longingly at them. "Yes." Even though we were restricted from having contact with our families until after the ceremony, he went over and whispered something to the kids, and they all ran over to give me a hug. It was so good to hold them, sharing with them the relief and pride of finishing this grueling year of training. This cadet's kind gesture still makes me smile.

For the commissioning ceremony, a diminutive female lieutenant colonel pinned my bar on one shoulder, and my son, Bobby, pinned on the other. I became Second Lieutenant (2LT) Carol Rogers. I was now an Army Leader. I was done practicing, but I found I would never be done learning.

After commissioning, I joined my unit for their second week of annual training at Fort Lee, Virginia. This was the same unit I belonged to as an enlisted soldier. I had a new assignment, but many of the people who were previously my peers were now my subordinates.

My first challenge came only days after my commissioning. I was assigned as Executive Officer (XO) to the Commander of Headquarters Company. It was difficult to go from the role of peer to one of being in charge, and I was uncomfortably conscious of a kind of tension.

I came into my office one morning and someone had defecated on my desk! A lump formed in the pit of my stomach. I was a nice person. People liked me. If this was a message, I didn't know what it was, but I knew it was not a welcome letter. I was disturbed and sick. I told my admin person to have it cleaned by the time I returned, and I left. I did not go to the Commander; I wanted to be alone. I never knew who was behind this, or what he (this was not done by a female) was trying to prove. This was a repercussion of moving forward with my life and my career, leaving others behind. I had to persist. There would undoubtedly be more instances when I would be challenged or provoked by others. I needed the "thicker skin" my mom referred to because not everyone was going to like me.

Those first couple months at drills continued to be difficult. I would tell someone to do something, and he or she tried to play the "buddy" card. Or others would treat me casually, not saluting or paying the respect we were trained at OCS to expect. It did not bother me in an informal situation, but I also knew my senior officers were judging me on how well I exercised authority and slipped into my new role as officer. I found myself in a balancing act between being a new officer with responsibility for my subordinates, and not becoming too full of myself and destroying the support I needed from the people who worked for me. It was difficult for me, and there were many challenges.

I turned to some of my fellow and senior officers for help and counseling. They shared with me their perspectives and struggles with their roles as officers (one officer was senior to a soldier who was his supervisor in their civilian job), and I was able to get coaching to deal with my new role. I also decided to have discussions with my subordinates regarding military customs and courtesies. I reminded them they must salute the rank, not necessarily the person. As an officer, I always strived to be someone my subordinates would want to salute, but this was not always the case. Thankfully, we eventually all settled into this new relationship.

There were some leadership incidents I was involved in as an officer I found particularly upsetting: First, I had this Battalion Commanding Officer (CO). He was a "nice guy," not a dynamic leader by any means, kind of dull and without much personality. Higher Headquarters sent a team to conduct an inspection of the Battalion. This is done periodically to evaluate the effectiveness of the unit, as well as the unit's readiness in the event of mobilization. On the last day of the inspection, the team called the CO along with his staff and proceeded to give the results of their inspection. Even though I was a new officer, I had been in this unit for three years prior, so I knew a little about the unit. It became painfully clear they were out to burn this commander. Many of the things written were ridiculous and were presented in a manner indicating minor infractions were serious offenses. However, even though he personally did not commit these infractions, as a Commander, he was responsible for what happened in his unit. After reading this bogus list of transgressions, they proceeded to relieve him of his command—in front of his whole staff. He wasn't a great leader, but he worked hard and believed in the Army, which he served. He did not deserve to be publicly denigrated. This was my first lesson in leadership, and it was sobering. A commander is always responsible for what happens in his unit, to the smallest detail—which is why he gets paid the big bucks. I also learned good intentions are not always recognized, and sometimes life is not fair. These lessons resonated with me throughout my career, especially when I saw other commanders making excuses and trying to shirk their responsibility.

The second thing I found upsetting concerned the Command Sergeant Major (CSM) who helped me get my paperwork together for OCS. Some of his actions came to the attention of higher headquarters and a new Battalion Commander was brought in to "look into things." At the time, I was assigned as Commander, Headquarters Company, and this CSM's son was one of the men in my company. One of my responsibilities was to sign the weekend drill statements, verifying who was present for drill. One weekend, the CSM's son did not show up for drill, and I marked him absent from drill and signed the form. I made a copy of the form, as instructed by the new CO. Every reserve unit has a full-time representative who takes care of administrative responsibilities during the weeks between drills. Our full-time administrative representative was the CSM, and one of his duties was to send out the weekend drill statement. The form sent out indicated his son was present. The CO compared the document sent out with the copy I had made and used this to build a case against the CSM. There were other transgressions, but as a result, the CSM was fired from the full-time position and was discharged from the US Army Reserves. He subsequently fought it and the charges were downgraded, but his career was ruined. This was upsetting because he was a good man, but he made some bad choices. I regretted being part of his undoing, especially since he had been such a big help to me when I wanted to go the officer route. But I had to separate my personal judgments from the situation at hand. It wasn't personal; there are consequences for bad choices. It helped to learn this perspective early, because later in my career there were times when I had to relieve, or fire someone. It was never easy, but learning to separate individuals from actions and consequences gave me clarity in these situations.

My training at OCS, along with my initial assignments in the Reserves and my attitudes as a result of my family of origin, shaped me as an officer and leader. The learning curve during those first few years was huge. I was stepping into a role I was meant for. I was learning and acquiring qualities which would provide for continued growth in my career and life. I had to accept my mistakes and learn from them. I saw others make mistakes and believe I learned from those as well. I also had to rely on the values and work ethic I learned from my parents to effectively be part of a team and a leader. Inherently, I knew it was the start of great things to come.

6

Persistence: Finding My Life Work

A big change was coming in my life, but I had no idea what it would be. I jumped from one idea to the next: I researched starting a catering company; next I was going to buy a house, or maybe I would get married. At the time, I had a relationship with potential. I became enthused about each of these possibilities, but none of these changes were what I needed, what I was searching for.

The same year I was commissioned, I also finished night school and received a second degree as a paralegal. I was lucky enough to find a paralegal job at a prestigious law firm in Buffalo, NY. I was working full time as a paralegal and part-time as a reserve officer attending monthly drills. However, after a couple years, I wanted more—a better life for the kids and for me. I again turned to my faith for discernment and direction. I prayed while I pursued different options. One personal event happened while I was working at the law firm. I met Jacqie, who was working there part-time while working on her master's degree. I quickly became good friends with her and her husband, and she was someone I shared much of my life with going forward.

It was nearing 3 years since I had been commissioned, and I had to get my Officer Basic Course (OBC) completed so I would be eligible for First Lieutenant (1LT). Many of the lawyers at the law firm where I worked were Navy officers who periodically took time off to go to school or perform duty. So, when I requested time off from work for my OBC for nine weeks, they willingly agreed. I found the Adjutant General Officer Basic Course (AGOBC) was due to start in one month. Adjutant General is the specialty that would prepare me to perform the administrative functions of a unit. I was excited and prepared to go off again for military training.

I was also considering that maybe the change I needed was another job. I loved the legal courses I took to earn my paralegal degree, and I liked working in a law firm, but there was no way I was going to get promoted to a lawyer. And I still didn't have the economic means for law school. So, I took exams for various federal agencies, including the Treasury Department and the Federal Bureau of investigation. The process for both was extremely long and detailed. So, while waiting for results, I hopped into my car and headed for Fort Benjamin Harrison in Indianapolis, Indiana, to attend my Officer Basic Course.

Classes were manageable, and they didn't require a lot of study. I found myself at a military school with much more time on my hands than I had at home working full time attending monthly drills, maintaining a household, and raising three kids.

There was a notice requesting soldiers to volunteer for the "Commander's Program." This program encouraged reservists to sign on for Active Duty. I considered this. I had received notice I was being considered for FBI Special Agent, pending a background investigation. I weighed the FBI against Active Duty. Both jobs entailed long days at work, and the pay was comparable. Another consideration was where my children and I would live. The FBI told me my chances were about 99% that my first job in the FBI would be NYC. There were no guarantees how close to work I could find housing. Whereas the military often provided family housing on the Army Post, and

I would never be too far from my kids and their schools. So, I told my supervisor I wanted to volunteer for the Commander's Program. He investigated it and informed me the Army policy precluded bringing a single parent with three children on Active Duty. Since I was only separated from Bob when I first joined the Army, I was still considered married. However, my divorce from him had become final, so now I was officially a single parent. This was distressing news because I was hopeful Active Duty was the career answer I was looking for. But at least I still had the FBI position.

I was at school on Easter, so my parents agreed to bring the kids to Fort Benjamin Harrison. I got a room for my parents, and the kids stayed with me. I could awake early with them to look for their Easter baskets, because of course the Easter Bunny could find them in Indiana.

I found there weren't a lot of places to hide Easter baskets in my small room, so I decided to hide them outside. The kids were awake and dressed to go basket hunting. It was a beautiful spring day in Indiana. The sun was shining, flowers were blooming, and the sky was blue. Military posts are beautiful places, well maintained and groomed. We were in our Easter outfits, as we planned to meet my parents for church and brunch after the baskets were found. The girls found theirs quickly. However, Bobby was younger and having a harder time. His basket was a little further away on the Parade Field. So, I gave him a hint, and he went running off to the Parade Field. When I got there, I found him on the grandstand crying. Someone or something had found his basket first. It was dumped out, ants all over the jellybeans, one whole chocolate rabbit missing and the other with teeth marks where the head used to be. This was a tactical error for this military mom. Bobby was devastated to find this disaster rather than an Easter basket of goodies. I looked on at his disappointment, already searching for ways to remedy the situation. However, the girls saw his disappointment and offered to share their candy with him. Soon we were all able to see some humor in the situation and laugh. We chuckled about the rabbit or squirrel who was sick to his stomach after eating all the chocolate.

I missed my kids when I was away and tried to include them in my life, wherever and whenever I could. They were at my commissioning, they participated in holiday parties at my reserve unit, and they came to Fort Ben Harrison to spend Easter with me. We were all enjoying (or at least exposed to) the different aspects of military life.

As I continued through the course, I was not ready to let go of the idea of Active Duty. I continued talking to my senior officers about the Commander's Program. Finally, I said, "Well, if the Army doesn't want me, let them tell me directly. I want to officially apply." This time, there was no shortage of help to get my application paperwork together. One instructor suggested that, as part of the packet, I write a letter explaining why the Army should bring me on Active Duty as a single parent of three. In my letter, I explained the life my children and I would like to have would not happen with a basic eight-hour-a-day job. I also commented that I had already shared many aspects of military life with my children, and we all respected the discipline of the Army, as well as the sense of loyalty to and respect for the country. Even though I wasn't the top of my class, it helped that I was in the top 10%. The Battalion Commander even wrote me a letter of recommendation to be included with my packet.

I was anxiously waiting, but did not hear anything. Finally, graduation day had almost arrived, and I was making plans to return home and get back to work. On the day before graduation, I got called to the Commandant's office. He admitted to me, "I didn't believe this would happen, but congratulations. You have been selected for Active Duty." I was elated. This was the big change in my life I had anticipated. I had no doubt of it. This also turned out to be the first in several instances the Army told me I couldn't do something, and I found a way to do it. It also shows how persistence, combined with faith, led me to this goal. This is especially noteworthy, since there were a number of people who had to approve my request: First, the Commander of my AGOBC Course had to sign off and give his recommendation. The Director of the Course had to do the same; also, the Commander of the US Army Soldier Support Center had to approve and sign off; followed by the Commandant of the US Army Institute of Personnel and Resource Management. Afterwards, the packet went to Commander, US Army Reserve Command Personnel Administration Center (USARCPAC), and finally to the active component, the Commander, US Military Personnel Center (USMILPERCEN), who made the final determination and approval. I know this sounds like a lot of military jargon, but this is how circuitous the approval process for this exception to policy was. This was a significant Army decision.

I found out at graduation, when they called my name, I was being assigned to Fort Bragg, NC. I requested Fort Bragg because I liked the location. At the time, I did not know Airborne from Chair-born, but I did know Ft. Bragg wasn't far from the ocean and this was good enough for me.

In my naivete, I planned to go home, take care of some things, let the kids finish school, maybe take a vacation, and casually proceed to Fort Bragg in a couple months. The Commander handed me my orders after graduation, and I had to report in two weeks. The Army backdated my entrance to active duty to March 6, 1981, the first day of my Office Basic Course, and gave me 2 weeks' leave at the end of the course, before reporting to Ft. Bragg. After graduating from AGOBC, I got in the car, drove straight through the night, and arrived home about 6 a.m. I woke my kids and sat with them. "I have three things to tell you: (1) I signed on for Active Duty in the Army. (2) We are moving to Fort Bragg and (3) we have to be there in two weeks." This was a lot for them to digest, but after answering their questions, they went off to school. I got dressed and went to work. I did not want to talk to my coworkers about my move until I told my boss. So, I had my secretary type my letter of resignation, giving 2 weeks' notice and taking my 2 weeks' vacation. Once the letter was written, I took it to my boss—the head of the Litigation Department. After I told him, one of the partners came in. He was a brilliant lawyer, who scuffled in his slipper-like shoes and looked like he slept in his clothes. My boss said, "Guess what, Al? Carol is quitting the firm and joining the Army." At which point Al slowly scuffled around the couch where we were sitting and sat, saying, "Somehow I don't feel any safer." I was not insulted. I always enjoyed this kind of "repartee" with men; it was funny.

I went to my children's school and made arrangements for them to finish the school year early so we could leave, and they would have their grades and move to the next grade. They were all good students, so it was not a problem. Next, I made arrangements with the movers to help us move to Ft. Bragg. I had moved a couple times before—but it was always on the cheap: hire a U-Haul, get boxes from the Grocery store, pack my stuff, and get my friends and family to come and load me. The contract movers for the Army told me to keep aside what I didn't want packed. The crew came in, and they packed everything, including the garbage can from the bathroom, which had not been emptied. This was a new and astonishing experience for me, and the beginning of a series of Army-initiated moves for my family. I knew this was the big change in my life I had prayed and worked for. We were all excited but anxious about this move. It was an adventure for all of us. I hoped my enthusiasm would spread to the kids, but they were sad to leave their friends and family. I promised we would call and talk to them regularly, and we would come home for holidays, hoping this would give them something to look forward to during this difficult transition. We were off to our next adventure, Fort Bragg, North Carolina.

7

Fort Bragg: Balancing Life as Soldier and Mother

Active Duty Army. This was a HUGE change for us. We would be living on an Army Post, with people in camouflage uniforms and military vehicles everywhere we turned, who stopped, came to attention, and saluted the flag every evening as it was lowered and TAPs was boomed through loudspeakers. This was a new world, intimidating yet intriguing for all of us.

We had military family housing, which offered a much greater sense of community than our old neighborhood. We would have our own house, relatively new, with a yard, which we immediately filled with a dog. Each of the kids could have their own room. Every house in our neighborhood had children of various ages. Arriving in the summer, there was no shortage of kids around, and they were all outside playing, and Kelly, Amy, and Bobby had the next three months to get acquainted with other kids and make friends. This would help them adjust. It was fortunate the three of them were so close in age, as they could support each other in socializing with other kids. In the fall Bobby started 5th grade and Amy and Kelly 7th and 8th grade respectively. By this time, they had met many other children and made some new friends.

This is not to say the transition was easy for them. They not only moved to a new neighborhood, where they did not know anyone, they had to move to another part of the country, start a new school without knowing a soul, and were separated from a large family support system, which was a significant part of their lives. There were no grandparents around the corner if mom had to work late. No cousins to play with a short drive away. However, on the flip side, they met other children who had the same experiences of having to leave family and friends, making new friends in a new location and in a new school. Family housing had a sense of community. We took care of one another and watched out for each other's kids. I had one neighbor who used to take Bobby running with him, while throwing a football for him to run and catch. This was one of the blessings of being in the Army. It was a kind of family for all of us. There was a camaraderie of living and working with people who also faced the challenges of moving regularly. So, our neighbors were adept at helping with the transition; people in the neighborhood were welcoming and helpful and the kids learned to share their concerns and how to adapt.

Years later, when attending college, my children commented they had an easier time acclimating to being away from home and having to make new friends and adjust to a new life than many of their classmates. To this day, we are still friends with families we met while living in military housing throughout my career. Kelly met her husband during one of my military assignments and all the kids have lifelong friends from this period of their life. I always tried to develop close relationships with the parents of my children's friends. I wanted to do social things with other families so my children could see what a committed relationship looked like, if I couldn't model it myself. So, in addition to aunts, uncles, and grandparents, we had military families we were close to. I hoped this would compensate for not having both parents themselves.

The kids were also exposed to the professionalism of the troops at Fort Bragg. This is home to the XVIII Airborne Corps and the 82d Airborne Division, the 1st Air Cavalry, the Special

Operations Command (Special Forces or Green Berets), and the Rangers. These are elite troop units who value professionalism and hard work. Since this was our first exposure to military life, the children saw firsthand, through our neighbors and their friend's families, a strong dedication to duty and a connection to one another. I mistakenly expected all Army bases had troops like those assigned to units at Ft. Bragg. I spent the rest of my career looking for this.

I was slotted to be the S-1 (the Adjutant—or administrative person—and part of the Commander's staff) in the 58th Air Traffic Control (ATC) Battalion, which was the parent unit for two other units. We provided air traffic control support to the 82d Airborne Division at Fort Bragg, the 101st Air Assault Division at Ft. Campbell, and the 24th Airborne Division at Ft. Stewart. The unit was composed of air traffic controllers (enlisted) and UH-1 helicopter pilots (officers). I loved these guys. They worked hard and played hard. I reported directly to the Executive Officer (XO), who welcomed me with, "I don't mind women in the military. . .as long as they perform as well as the men." He emphatically added, "By the way, we have a Post run once a month—4 miles at an 8 minute-mile pace, and I expect my officers to lead." This might not sound daunting to you, but to someone who squeezed through her two-mile run at my annual Army Physical Fitness Tests, this was a little formidable. So, I immediately started training. There was a running course which was part of our physical training (PT) called the Mata-Mile. This was a 4.34-mile course partly on pavement, but mostly a track, through the woods with a total incline of 238 feet. During one run, while I was huffing and puffing, trying to make it up a particularly steep incline, a soldier went running past me. Now this was not especially noteworthy, but he was in full uniform, including boots AND a rucksack. But the clincher was he also had a lit cigarette hanging from his mouth. I was ready to throw my hands in the air and give up. But this was one of the beauties of Ft. Bragg.

At any time of the day or night, you could look outside and see some incredible specimen of the human race outside running. It seemed EVERYONE was into physical fitness.

My job in the 58th ATC Battalion covered all aspects of personnel management and administration. The XO who, despite his first skeptical remarks about female soldiers, gradually seemed to accept me and ultimately helped me in my transition to active-duty military. The XO was a boss you love to hate. He was so authentic; you saw all his foibles as well as his good qualities. So, when it was time for him to rotate out of this assignment, I organized a roast in his honor. And there was no shortage of material to work with. He was especially noted for looking in people's desk drawers throughout the day. He believed your desk was the property of the Army, therefore it was not your private possession. One of the comments at his roast was, "Major Klink initiated a new and effective way of distributing useful information—simply leave it in your top desk drawer." The event was an evening of fun and laughter. Despite the roast being full of sarcasm and pointing out all his mannerisms we would not miss, it was also recognition of his dedication to duty and how seriously he took his role in the unit. The XO did not feel criticized. He enjoyed the jokes as much as everyone else. I was at home in this environment of teasing and repartee, and I could give as well as receive; this led to acceptance in this predominantly male army.

As a staff member, I was required to make periodic staff visits to Ft. Campbell and Ft. Stewart. The 58th ATC Battalion had helicopters, so this was the mode of transportation we used. I had never flown in a helicopter before, so the first trip I made caught me by surprise. I was in the back seat next to the door, and it was a beautiful summer day. It was warm, the sky was blue, and the sun was shining. As we proceeded to take off, I waved frantically to the pilot that he had forgotten to close the door. Everyone burst into laughter, and no one seemed concerned at all. They patiently explained the centrifugal force would hold me in the helicopter, and I would not fall out. However, despite all their assurances, I was not convinced a strong gust of wind wouldn't "WHOOSH" come and swoop me out! Ironically, I found I loved flying. I enjoyed being in anything that flew, and I had some unique opportunities at Ft. Bragg. The Commander was issued a T-42 aircraft (a small 4-seater fixed wing plane) we sometimes traveled in. Additionally, one of the Staff Officers flew an old Army "bird dog," pulling advertisements at Myrtle Beach in the summer. He took me for a ride one day and did somersaults in the sky. I loved it. There was something about the sense of freedom while flying around in the sky. I could leave all my worries and troubles on the ground. I was lighter.

Since my original attraction to Fort Bragg was the proximity to the ocean, the kids and I often took advantage of it. We would often awake at 6 a.m. on a Saturday, load the car, and head for the beach. We arrived about 9, in time for breakfast on the beach. We would spend the day playing in the ocean and relaxing on the beach. My favorite time of day at the beach is about 4 p.m., when most of the sunbathers have left, the beach is quieter, the sun not as strong, and for some reason the power and vastness of the ocean, with the waves rushing in, is even more present to me. We would often walk the beach, enjoying the tranquility of the whole experience. Once my friend Jacqie, along with her husband and kids, traveled to North Carolina and joined us for a weekend at the beach. Sometimes, the kids would bring a friend. A few times we rented a house for the weekend; once with a family from Ft. Bragg, Bill and Therese Maasch, who we met early on, who had two girls, Beth and Marie and a boy, Billy, around the same ages as Kelly, Amy, and Bobby. They are one of the families we remain friends with to this day. Once we all went out for pizza, and I watched Billy and Bobby at the jukebox, picking out a tune. They were both wiry, thin boys with blond hair and freckles; there they were next to each other, with their skinny little butts moving back and forth to the music. The four girls were all young and beautiful, knockouts in their bathing suits and embarking on their teenage years, although Beth, who was the oldest, was ahead of the others. We loved the beach so much that one year we rented a condo at the beach for a week. The Maasch kids came with us. On the first day, Bobby broke a bone in his foot playing on a boogie board and the doctor put his foot in a cast. He was restricted from the beach for the rest of our stay. But faithful Billy stayed in the house all week with Bobby. He was that kind of friend.

The kids and I would take a vacation every year to go back to see relatives in Buffalo. I remember one Friday. I had to work that day, but had everything packed and ready when I got home. We loaded the car and took off. It was about a 10-hour ride to Buffalo from Ft. Bragg, and we were only about two hours in, and I was so exhausted. I pulled into a rest area and immediately fell asleep. I must have been sleeping a couple hours, when the kids woke me, saying, "Are we EVER going to Grammie and Umpie's (which is what all the grandkids called my parents)?" Those two hours restored me, and I hit the road and completed the trip. As much as we loved those trips, it was always so difficult to leave. As we would pull out of the driveway, my mom would be crying, my kids would be crying, and I was crying. One time, we got about 2 miles away, and I forgot my purse. So, we went back to get it. We said our goodbyes again, but this time there was only sadness, no tears. We set out again, and I got as far as the thruway entrance, and I had a flat tire. I called my dad, and he came and fixed it, along with my mom who came for the ride. By the time we finally left, there were no tears, no sadness, only resolve, "So when are we leaving?" Wow. If you have multiple goodbyes, it gets easier every time. When my time comes, this is how I would like to go.

Social life in the Army also included Happy Hours on Friday. Everyone went—the whole unit, plus spouses. There was a little, all ranks Club on Smoke Bomb Hill where we all went, listened to music, danced, and had a few drinks. All the disagreements we had with someone during the week were discussed and forgotten. Problems were solved and issues were resolved. Camaraderie was established at those Happy Hours. We got to know each other's spouses, and we got to know each other in a relaxed atmosphere.

Additionally, the 58th ATC Battalion offered many opportunities for family events. We enjoyed holiday gatherings and picnics. My kids got to know and interact with members of my unit as well as their children, some of whom were their age. The Commander was LTC Emmet Johnson, who I adored. He was a quiet, southern man who seemed genuinely interested in the troops working for him. He and his wife "adopted" the kids and me and would often invite us over for hamburgers or homemade ice cream. Also, they would host parties, some of which I was invited to as a member of his staff. I deduced, "If all I have to do to make rank is to throw a lot of parties, I can do this." Of course, I would soon learn there was way more to it than just throwing parties.

Prior to my decision to go on active duty, I was supporting three kids on a meager paralegal salary. Now, with housing included, I was making double the money. I no longer had to save for a month or two to get a new pair of jeans for one of the kids. I could buy some new beds and furniture. At the time, families could use the military dental facilities on Post, and Amy and Bobby were able to get the braces and retainer (respectively) that they needed. We were rich.

The Army has a system for promotions: If you get "passed over" for promotion two times, you will be released from active duty. To be competitive for promotions, you had to have jobs providing experience and variety in your area of expertise. So, as much as I loved being the administrative staff officer of the 58th ATC Battalion, after a while, it was time to move on, get another assignment, get some more experience to be competitive for promotions. I started looking for other open administrative positions on post where I might transfer. My search brought me to a lot of options, including the Special Operations Command at Ft. Bragg. Finally, I accepted an assignment at XVIII Airborne Corps, Manpower Readiness Division. This was another administrative job, but this time working with Corps, which is a much higher level of command.

Soon after arriving at my new assignment at Corps, I was eligible for promotion to captain. There was another female lieutenant who worked in Corps administration who also came out on the promotion list. Since we both had the same senior supervisor, who would be performing the promotion, he decided to do a joint ceremony. I was still relatively new to the Army. I didn't know ceremonies and promotions were a big deal. So, all I did was get someone to bring my kids to the ceremony. I was no longer with all the folks I knew at the 58th ATC Battalion, and not with the Corps long enough to have established friendships there; so, I didn't invite anyone. However, unbeknownst to me, the woman being promoted with me had been at Corps for almost 3 years and was married to a LTC who was a battalion commander in the 82nd Airborne Division (a subunit of Corps). So, imagine my surprise when I came into the promotion ceremony and the hall was packed. And imagine my disappointment when everyone was there for her. This was a humbling experience, but I still walked away wearing the rank of captain in the Army.

I was single and enjoyed dating in the Army. I introduced my kids to anyone I was dating. I remember I was dating one man, and he stood me up for a date. When he called to apologize (something about being called into work—he was with the 1st Air Cavalry), he invited me over for the afternoon. At first I said, "No way." But I reconsidered. "Sure, I'll be there in half an hour." I proceeded to load my kids and their friends into my car and headed to his place. Having five kids running around his bachelor pad, playing with his pool table and foosball table was not what he had in mind for this Sunday afternoon. But he was great about it and joined in the fun, and we had a great afternoon.

XVIII Airborne Corps taught me a lot as a young captain. I had to visit all the subordinate units to assess their personnel status, noting the critical shortages impacting mission effectiveness. I had to complete a monthly readiness report and brief it to the three-Star Commanding General. The report had to be succinct, accurate, and perfectly written; it went through numerous reviews and revisions before I briefed it. My job allowed me to learn firsthand the impact of shortages on the unit's ability to deploy in support of a national emergency. Additionally, it was beneficial as a low-grade officer to have the experience of briefing a three-star General, which was extremely intimidating; I remember being nervous and anxious. But I learned that if I knew the material (which I did after all the preparation and reviews) I was able to answer most questions. I recall the first time I did not know the answer to a question, something about a disparity in numbers between last month and this month. My mind was racing—could I have copied the numbers wrong? No, the numbers had gone through too many reviews. Was there an incident (influx of people coming in or out of the unit) that would explain it? Finally, I had to admit I did not have the answer, but I told him I would investigate it and get back to him. This was difficult for me. It was humbling. I HAD to have the answers. In the long run, I saved myself more embarrassment by being honest. Moreover, the Army allowed young officers the opportunity to use these situations to learn and broaden their scope.

Most personnel positions in Corps were "jump slots," meaning you had to be airborne qualified to be in the position. Additionally, you had to jump once a quarter to maintain your jump status. My immediate supervisor at Corps was a Lieutenant Colonel. He was a hard-working, serious boss. The thing I remember most about my supervisor was he loved to jump, and being part of the Corps. However, every morning before a jump, he would go to the latrine and vomit. Yes, sick to his stomach. Every time. I suspect he had to be stressed or even fearful, but he jumped anyway. This was the dedication and quality of people I worked with; I loved working with them.

There was something contagious about being in an Airborne Unit, like the greetings exchanged. One person would call out, "All the Way," and the soldier's response was "Airborne." I had to go to jump school.

The Army uses training exercises to test the readiness of a unit or to test plans and strategies. When I was first assigned to the 58th ATC Battalion, exercises would be scheduled, but I was never slotted to go. When I discussed this with my Commander, he confessed he wanted to help me, since I would have to make arrangements for the kids. I told him this was an experience I needed to have. I didn't want to be a Commander myself someday and never been to the field for an exercise. I wanted to have this experience as a young officer when there was more room for mistakes, rather than as a Commander. From this point on, I was included in field exercises. I second-guessed my request when, at my first exercise, I crawled out of my sleeping bag in my cold tent, got dressed, ate my Meal,Ready-to-Eat (MRE), and moved out to the pouring rain to perform my functions. But ultimately, I knew I made the right decision. I was part of a team.

Various troops at Ft Bragg were always having exercises. I specifically remember one exercise at Ft. Irwin, CA. Many units sent representatives out for this exercise, and part of the exercise was jumping into the exercise area. When the units of the 82d Airborne Division were due to jump, there was a bad wind blowing. Standard procedure requires a Warrant Officer on the ground, a meteorologist, who monitors the wind gusts and reports when they are higher than safety precautions will allow, making it unsafe to jump. However, it is the Exercise Commander who makes the final call. At this point, I had been around these Airborne types long enough to visualize how it happened: the meteorologist reported the unsafe winds to the Exercise Commander. The Exercise Commander looked around, decided his guys were tough airborne troops and made the determination they could handle it, and ordered the jump to commence. However it happened, the gusts were so high that when the Airborne troops landed, their parachutes were caught in the wind and they were dragged along the ground, some to their death. There was an investigation and in the final determination, the fault landed on the shoulders of the poor warrant officer, but there are some higher-ranking officers carrying this guilt to their graves.

The night of the exercise, my kids came home from school and shared that their classmates were all talking about the exercise; they all knew someone from school whose father had been killed in the exercise, by jumping in high winds. They learned not only could soldiers die in a war, but they could also die in an exercise, doing their job. As much as I enjoyed the bravado of the hard-core troops at Ft. Bragg, this is an example where it replaced a healthy caution. It is amusing and entertaining to have a boastful and cocky attitude about your unit being the best, and it creates unity and Esprit de Corps for its members. However, an element of rationality needs to be maintained when it comes to people's lives. We rely on our senior leaders to adhere to this. It is demoralizing when they don't.

Exercises prepare us for a real engagement such as the invasion of Grenada in 1983. The US invaded Grenada to restore democracy after the internal problems of the People's Revolutionary Government. Responding to pleas from the Organization of Eastern Caribbean States and the Governor-General of Grenada, the United States, under President Reagan, decided to launch a military intervention. I was assigned to XVIII Airborne Corps at the time. Units were put on alert, and a group went out as part of the first wave. I was identified as part of the second wave, and as such, I had to prepare for deployment.

It was time to put the Dependent Care Plan I had written

years ago to the test. My plan designated my parents to take care of my children. I had two options: transport my children to my parents' house in Buffalo, or bring my parents to my home, which was preferable if it was during the school year. I planned for logistics and made arrangements for their expenses. This was a requirement for any parent soldier, whether married or single. As it turned out, the crisis in Grenada was resolved and I never did have to deploy. However, the whole procedure was a sobering wake-up call for potential situations which could arise in the future. I didn't discuss this with my children, not wanting to worry them unless deployment was imminent. I had made plans impacting their lives, but other than making them aware of the plans, we didn't have an in-depth discussion about it. They must have had questions. "Who will stay with us until Grammie and Umpie come? How long will this last? Will we be able to talk to mom?" and any number of other questions. And what about the impact of their mom going off to a warzone? I recently probed Bobby about it, and he responded, "I don't remember it at all. I was used to you going off to training at different points in your career and figured this would be another time you would be gone."

As much as I tried to be a good mom, I made mistakes. I loved my kids, and I loved being a mother. I wanted my career, but my children were always behind the major decisions I made. I was trying to make a better life for them and believed the career choices I made would ultimately bring them to a good place. However, despite my best efforts, I was overwhelmed trying to deal with teenagers by myself. My kids were getting older; during our three years at Ft. Bragg, the girls were going through their pre-teen and teen years, going through puberty, experiencing the raging hormones accompanying this process, and my kids needed a more present parent figure in their life, especially my daughters. At the same time, I enjoyed dating. I rationalized running a household, being the sole breadwinner, and raising three children on my own was stressful. I was often overwhelmed, trying to balance everything. "With everything on my plate…", I justified, "I had a right to date, to go out and have a good time." I became a "serial monogamist". I had a lot of relationships but only one man at a time. When one relationship was over, it was time to move on. At the time I did not see dating as a problem—it was the '80s. The pill had given women a new sense of freedom, and it seemed all the single women I knew were enjoying this freedom. I wasn't ashamed of my life, but I was more open than I should have been with my kids. The disagreements between the girls and me were normal frictions between teens and parents. They were testing my authority as well as pushing the limits I had set for them. They were all trying to make sense of their lives. I remember talking to a couple who were friends of mine, and they advised, "You need to keep talking. Find a way to talk." But what I needed was to "Listen." My own parents never modeled active listening, and I never learned to listen, believing in the old school idea that the parent's word is final. I sought counseling, prayed, and turned to other couples to deal with my kids. It wasn't until later the issue of my going out and having boyfriends arose. Amy specifically was especially verbal about her resentment. Looking back, I can clearly see how this negatively impacted my daughters. My sons didn't seem to have a problem with it.

This is why it is so crucial for children to have two parents, so the parents can offset one another, bringing in different perspectives. The only perspective my children had was mine—how I wanted things to be done.

Kelly was a smart, sensitive child. She was pretty. And as the oldest child, she was responsible. She exuded a sense of confidence which belied some hidden insecurities and worries about failing. She was the peacemaker in the family and always tended to be there to mediate between her siblings or between them and me. She developed physically at a young age and was confused by the conflict this created. Her grandfather and uncles who used to roll around and play with her as a child now were hesitant and more stand-off-ish. "How to deal with a child who is now in a woman's body?" She seemed to sense this, but was baffled by these changes. As she grew older, her confidence was often seen as aloofness by her male peers, making her even more attractive and elusive to the boys in her classes, and she never was short of boys to date. She always had an eye for sweet, considerate boys to bring home to meet mom. One of the first boys she dated at Ft. Bragg brought ME a rose on his first date with Kelly.

However, Kelly and I were clashing a lot during this time. She was not a bad kid, a normal teen, questioning authority. And, as much as I hate to admit it, I was a screamer, as my mom was. I write this calmly now, but I cannot discount the impact on my kids of having a crazy woman for a mom. One night Kelly and I had a particularly heated argument, and I told her, "Pack your bags. I am sending you to live with your father. I'll have a plane ticket tonight." As Kelly stoically packed her bag, Amy was crying and begging me not to send her sister away. When we got in the car to leave, I turned around to the kids, but especially Kelly, and said, "Sending you away would be like cutting off my arm. There is no way I could ever do this. But I am so frustrated, I don't know what to do anymore." We all quietly went back into the house. I wish I did more of this—shared more with the kids. Also listened more to them. It had taken until this point in my life to listen and be in their world and to try to address and apologize for my shortcomings. After the incident, Kelly changed. Our relationship improved; at least the constant fighting stopped. I attribute it all to Kelly's efforts to accept me. This was a time when listening could have helped. It was an opportunity for both of us to discuss what was going on and how we could more effectively move forward. Regrettably, at the time, I did not have those tools or this insight. I was doing the best I could, but sometimes it simply wasn't enough.

When I look back on raising my children as a single mom, I can see how short-tempered I was, how hot-headed I could be. I pulled myself together and went to work, calm and controlled. How would it have been if it was reversed: if I was calm and controlled at home and a hot head at work? It would have been incredible for the kids, could have made a huge difference in their life, but not so sure about work. I have seen some hot-head male officers move ahead in rank, but a hot-headed female officer would not have made the cut. If my military or any other career was impacted by my temper, how would I have supported my family? This is all conjecture.

Also, I was singularly supporting my family. I received only $100 a month from Bob in child support for three kids until they turned 18. (This, a statement of the court's responsiveness to single moms!) I was responsible for obtaining and maintaining a home (including repairs and cleaning), I was responsible for buying food, preparing meals, seeing we were well nourished. I was responsible for choosing, paying for, and maintaining a mode of transportation. I was responsible for the welfare and wellbeing of my children, nursing them when they were sick, taking them to the doctor, getting them to school, attending parent-teacher meetings and school events, chauffeuring them to social events, cheering at their extra-curricular activities, making sure holidays and birthdays were celebrated. I was responsible for teaching them the value of hard work, caring for others, taking them to church, and so much more. I could delegate repairs, cleaning, etc., but ultimately, I was responsible. They received only occasional phone calls and visits from their father. He was living in the Midwest, and it did not result in any emotional support from him. In addition, I had a job that came with its own set of responsibilities. Obviously, one person cannot do it all without impacting some areas of their life; regrettably, it was my children who received the lion's share of the impact.

8

Debate: Women on the Battlefield

"Send that female captain home!" This was the response of the Battlefield Commander, when in 1983, at the onset of Grenada, a female captain (the one who had been promoted with me earlier, now a company commander with the 82d Airborne Division) landed in Grenada with her unit in the first wave. The Commander did not want women on the battlefield or in a warzone. The battlefield commander is the King of the Battlefield. So, she was sent home. This raised the issue of women in combat, which, apparently, had not previously been addressed.

After the Grenada conflict ended, there was a committee/panel formed to address the issue of women in combat, and I was part of a team to research and to make recommendations. I found the topic fascinating, once all aspects of it were considered. There are countries where women are combatants (Israel, Turkey) or historical female warriors (St. Joan of Arc and the female Amazons). But except as nurses, US female soldiers traditionally did not serve in combat units. However, once the Women's Army Corps was eliminated and women were absorbed into the regular Army, they filled slots in combat units, such as Administration or logistics. This was how a female was selected as a company commander in an infantry unit. After the incident in Grenada, the discussions continued throughout the Armed Forces without resolution until 1994, when women were officially excluded from combat. This meant they could not hold combat specialties, such as infantry, armor, artillery, and, later, combat aviation. Every position in the Army, from the lowest member of the unit to the Commander is coded. The code designates the grade (rank) and specialty (intelligence, armor, signal, infantry, etc.) Traditionally, promotions came faster to combat specialty soldiers and senior commanders (those of Corps and Field Armies). Three and four-star generals were always members of the combat arms. However, as shown by the example of the female company commander who deployed with her unit, women were requesting and gaining entrance into various positions in combat arms units not requiring a combat specialty.

Finally, in 2013, women were officially allowed to enter the combat arms specialties. It was recognized that battlefields no longer consisted of our front lines facing enemy front lines, as seen in WWI and WWII. There are no more "front lines" per se. Administrative and logistical centers could be targeted. Convoys could be ambushed. In a war, there were no safe places for members of a unit to reside. Perimeters could be reinforced, but the battlefield was everywhere. However, prior to 2013, 144 female soldiers died in combat in Iraq, Afghanistan, and Kuwait, despite not officially being assigned to a combat position. They took the same battle risks as their male combat arms peers, but male combat arms soldiers received awards as combatants (Combat Infantry Badge) and the female soldiers were not eligible. As a country we did a great disservice to these women who died in combat by not acknowledging them as combatants, regardless of Army verbiage and classifications.

Our team discussed various perspectives and issues, although many seem moot now in hindsight, since women can now serve in combat positions. However, it is still relevant to review them and all female soldiers seeking a combat specialty should consider them.

As we sat at the table on the first day, the most obvious objection to women in combat specialties was raised: women are not as strong as men. The doctor on the panel informed us, "It has been proven some women are indeed stronger than the average man. If motivated, they can train to become as strong as their male counterparts, and some may succeed. However, it is questionable whether they can sustain the physical demands of combat over a prolonged length of time." A discussion ensued about the merit of the last statement, and someone suggested the mental and emotional strength of women might compensate for extended physical demands. The doctor added, "Studies show the female body may be more prone to injuries than their denser-boned male counterparts." This was a consideration, but one which needed to be tracked and researched further.

I raised the issue about deep-seated male attitudes toward their female counterparts having nothing to do with a woman's ability to do the job. We agreed most men have a need to protect a female. Someone chimed in with this example: What if, in a combat situation, a male soldier is so concerned about the female next to him he can't leave her to do her job and trust she has his back? This may change over time, but what if his protectiveness keeps him from effectively performing his mission? It has nothing to do with the capability of the female soldier, but a man's own preconceived notions. This is something needing to be addressed and discussed within a unit. Someone else suggested even if the Army helps men overcome these pre-conceived attitudes, society has difficulty accepting the torture, maiming, raping, and death of a female in combat. How will the Army deal with that?

The most heated and controversial objection was sex. In the existing heterosexual army, there was the issue of intimate relationships forming. Despite fraternization policies, this cannot always be eliminated. In a peacetime army, there are more options than there would be if this happened in a deployed combat unit. If these relationships occur in a war-zone, it could cause distraction, caused by emotions, jealousy or worry by both the female and/or male members involved about their loved one. Someone else added, "And you can't discount the possibility of pregnancy. A unit trains to depend on each member doing his part to accomplish the mission. If after deployment, a female becomes pregnant, she simply is not able to accomplish her mission, resulting in a hole in the unit's integrity." One would hope if a woman worked as hard as necessary to get into a combat position, she would protect herself against getting pregnant. However, this is not guaranteed.

The panel went back and forth on these issues. We had to weigh facts against human behavior, good intentions against possible outcomes. We agreed there was no easy solution and any change would have to be implemented over time.

People often ask me what my personal opinion is about women in combat. I believe women should have equal opportunities in the military. But a female soldier should not make the decision lightly. She should give serious consideration to the points delineated above. Before putting her life on the line, she should be aware of the risk not only to herself, but also to her family. But if she decides to move forward, she should not get or expect special consideration because of her gender. And finally, she should strive to be a good soldier, not a good female soldier, in the Army. There is a difference.

9

Determination:
Fear Is No Excuse

Finally, as we stood in formation, on my 37th birthday, my name was called, and I was selected for jump school. This was after a grueling morning of selection and training. They had 240 soldiers vying for about 90 slots. So off I went for qualification. There was a standard Army Physical Fitness Test (APFT) for jump school. We all had the same number of pushups, sit-ups and running requirements, regardless of age or sex. As I waited to take my APFT, I saw these big, muscular men doing their pushups and the cadre counting, "Three. Four. Four. Four. . ." meaning their pushups were bad and weren't being counted. With so many applicants and so few slots, it became obvious they were using the APFT as the disqualifier, and they were judging the events strictly. I was shaken. There was no way I was going back to my unit and telling them I failed the APFT. When I moved to the front of the line for my pushups and the APFT, I was Army Strong. I was whipping those pushups out, till the instructor stopped me. "You have enough." But I did one more, simply to make sure. I finished the sit-ups, and set out for my next obstacle, the two-mile run: in uniform and boots, in 16 minutes. Of course, by this time I had been running the monthly Corps run, which was four miles in 32 minutes, so I was good to go. The boots may have slowed me, but I was running on adrenaline now and finished the run in record time. The cadre called us together and told us to have lunch and report back at 1300 hours for "Orientation." I excitedly stopped by my unit to tell them I qualified for jump school and all we had in the afternoon was orientation. So, I planned to meet them at 1600 hours for drinks at happy hour. Boy, was I in for a surprise.

The "orientation" consisted of letting us know this was not a gentleman's course. Because I was an officer, I was assigned as stick leader. This meant I was responsible for the 10 soldiers in my stick. If they did something causing them to be dropped for push-ups, I joined them. I taped my long hair on my head. Can't have any loose hair getting caught in a cable. The cadre whipped us into shape. "Give me 20 push-ups." "Run to the outer fence." "Drop for 20." "Run back to this Jumpmaster." "10 pull-ups." "Double-time round the field." When we had no energy left, and were dripping with sweat, they called us over for a break. They directed us to a dugout and proceeded to hose us, creating a lot of mud. In the middle of this mess, they dropped us for push-ups again. And the fun started all over again. Around 1800 (long after happy hour had started) we were released. With the sweat and the mud and the fatigue and my taped hair, you can imagine how I looked. This was jump school, June 22, 1984. As I left, I passed one of the cadres and commented that this was no way to treat a lady on her birthday.

I dragged my weary body home, and as I arrived home, one of my neighbors noticed me, "What in God's name happened?" I told him this evening I finished jump school orientation, and he knowingly burst out laughing as he called to all the other neighbors, "Hey, everybody. Look. Carol started jump school today." At which point there was a whole lot more whooping and laughing. But it didn't matter; I knew I was on my way to becoming a part of this elite group of Airborne soldiers.

The next day, it was time for serious training. I soon found out yesterday's "orientation" was child's play. First, we had to be outfitted. We did all our training, running, and drills in full gear. It was summer at Ft. Bragg, but for jump school, our sleeves were rolled down, even though the temperature was in the eighties. We wore 30-pound rucksacks, to get used to the weight of our parachutes, and we trained with our helmets. After a couple days, my neck was black and blue from the weight on my back and head. Mornings started out with a physical training routine—pushups, sit-ups, and running. The academic training included the aerodynamics of our parachutes, as well as the use of toggles to steer the chute. We learned how to exit the aircraft, and how to avoid hazards when we were landing (trees, water, power lines, pavement, other parachutists), how to test if our chute opened, and how to open our back-up chute if needed. But the most intense training came with practicing parachute-landing falls (PLFs). We would have to stand on stages erected about 20 feet high (though maybe the height increased in my mind over the years) and we would have to fall off the stage sideways, learning to fall in a way to protect our bodies from the impact. It didn't take long before my body was black and blue. It took everything I could muster to get my weary body into my car, drive home to shower, and roll into bed at the end of the day. While I'm dragging myself home, my younger classmates were at the local bars, drinking and doing PLFs off the bar tables. Oh, the joys of youth!

The final phase of learning to jump concluded with the 34-foot tower. We were required to jump out of a mock airplane 34 feet high onto a static line, so we could experience our chute opening and jerking us. We needed five "Go's" from the 34-foot tower before we could move on to jump week. The drill was to climb the stairs, stand in the doorway of the mock aircraft, call out our name, rank, and roster number, and jump out, ensuring we clear the sides of the aircraft. I am in line with my stick, climbing the stairs, get in the doorway, yell out my info, jump, ride the line to the bottom, get unhooked by the cadre, double time over to the jumpmaster, report with my name, rank, and roster number and get his ruling. "No-Go! Double-time to the top of the line and do over." So off I go, double-timing past everyone slowly climbing the stairs, get in the doorway, call out my info, jump, ride the line, get unhooked, race back to the jumpmaster and again, "No-Go! Double-time to the top of the line and do it again." Well, I had a couple more No-Go's and one of the cadres took me aside to work with me on my exits, explaining procedures and doing some drills. I tried again. "No-Go! Double-time to the top of the line and do over." So, I did a few more and received a few more No-Go's. I was taken aside and did some more drills, practicing the exit strategy. I couldn't figure out what I was doing wrong, but I kept trying. By 8:00 at night, I had 32 No-Go's in a row. The school Sergeant Major came over and intervened. "She is thoroughly fatigued. She can't do anymore. Send her home for today. Let her come back tomorrow and try again."

At night I was talking to my kids on the phone. They were with my parents while I was at jump school. I told them about my day, cried about how discouraged, exhausted, and bruised I was. I talked to my mom and told her I wanted the kids to come to my graduation. Though at the time, I was not even sure I would make it. She complained, "Carol, you are talking 700 miles." I agreed but told her my kids heard how difficult the training was for me. If I graduated and earned my wings, I wanted them to see what success looks like. I wanted them to see the elation on my face, having done the impossible. I wanted them to want the same feeling for themselves someday.

So, I went back the next morning to tackle the 34-foot tower again. First time: "Go." Second time: "Go." Should I try for three? "Go." And "Go." on four, and finally fifth try and another "Go." I was moving on to jump week. Years later, I was relating this story to a Special Forces friend of mine, and he smiled, "They only wanted to see how bad you wanted it." I responded, "You're kidding me?" This never occurred to me at the time—I was frustrated because I couldn't get it right. My attitude served me better in the long run. Had I adopted the excuse it was because I was a female, or because I was an officer or because they wanted to see how badly I wanted it, I might not have tried so hard. I personally took responsibility and kept trying. Persistence. This worked for me.

Finally, it was jump week. To get my wings, I needed to make five jumps. If I broke my neck on the last one, I'd still get my wings. They would slap them on my dead body in the drop zone. If I could move on to the plane for my fifth jump, I would get my wings, even if they had to throw me off. So, I prayed for four good jumps. We had one jump a day for the whole week, culminating with the fifth jump and graduation on Friday.

Monday came and it was time for my first jump. I remember it was a beautiful summer day in North Carolina. The sun was shining, and the sky was blue. We had to report at 0400—but who could sleep anyway? We practiced a couple PLFs, received our briefings: what to do if you are heading toward power lines, or water, or pavement, or the trees; what to do if you get tangled in someone else's chute. One chute on top of another takes away the air it needs to stay open and could cause the lower one to collapse. The chutes we used are not the large, colorful square chutes you see skydivers performing with. Oh, no. These were the old canopy style chutes, steered with two toggles and took a lot of practice to control.

Finally, it's time to board the aircraft—a C-130. It's now about 0700 and a beautiful, still day. Military aircraft have no noise insulation like commercial planes do. All you can hear is the loud roar of engines. Also, instead of big, reclining seats, the seats are strips of canvas along the side. So, it is loud and uncomfortable, especially with a parachute strapped to your back. And I was scared to death. You know the terror that runs through you when someone sneaks behind you and scares you? I was in such a suspended state of terror for the whole ride to the drop zone. And despite this, I fell asleep. Do you believe it? I fell asleep. Finally, we were over the drop zone. There are multiple planes, each having two sticks on the right side of the plane, and two sticks are on the left side. So, when the first airplane makes its first pass, the first stick stands, hooks up to the static line and moves to the door. In fact, there is a marching song about this: "Stand up. Hook up. Shuffle to the door." I was the first person on the first stick of the first side of the first pass of the first plane. I was the first person in the whole class to jump.

The Jump Master called for the first stick, so we proceeded forward. The door of the aircraft was open, and I had to stand in the door. There was a small red light to my left and when it was clear to jump, it turned green. As I was standing in front of the door, I was told, "Don't look down." Now, I ask you when you are in the open door of an aircraft, where are you supposed to look? I noticed the light had turned green, and I heard a voice, far, far away in the distance say, "Jump!" "He can't possibly mean me." I again heard the voice, "Jump!" and I am not sure, but I may have gotten a nudge out the door with someone's boot. Suddenly, I was in total silence, under a beautiful blue summer sky, floating peacefully to the ground. It was the most incredible experience I have ever had. We were trained at jump school to count to 5, look to make sure our chute had opened, but honestly, I never had to. I always saw the other, heavier jumpers falling faster than me. I descended to the ground, wishing I had more time to float around the skies. When it was time, I did a textbook PLF, gathered my chute and headed off the field. I had completed my first jump. Four more to go and I would have earned my jump wings.

The second jump was okay, but on the third jump, I got tangled in another jumper's chute on the way down. If a chute came over me and I got tangled with someone else, I could lose the air in my chute. The ground was quickly approaching, eliminating the possibility of opening my backup chute, so I was working hard to get disentangled from the other chute.

I didn't have time to prepare a good PLF and I remember dropping hard on the ground. I was knocked out because I remember regaining consciousness, "Okay, let's move my toes. Yes, they move, how about my legs, my arms, yes. Turn my head. Okay, I'm fine. Stand and get going."

The fourth jump was our equipment jump. In addition to jumping with our 30-pound parachute, we also had to have a rucksack filled with 30 pounds of gear. At the time, I weighed 100 pounds, so I was carrying about two-thirds my body weight in gear. But hey, I was hard-core. They weighed my rucksack to make sure it was 30 pounds, and if I was short, they added a couple rocks. Thank goodness they did not check my rucksacks, because I am sure I would have been dropped for push-ups. In my rucksack was a beautiful, furry teddy bear. He made the jump with me and now he is an Airborne Teddy Bear, also sporting jump wings, now safely in the hands of Amy's daughter, my granddaughter. Fourth jump completed. Now we moved on to our last jump and graduation.

All along, I had been praying, "Dear God, please give me four good jumps." No matter what happens on your fifth jump, you get your wings. But I wanted to revise my prayer: "Dear God, can we renegotiate? I'd like FIVE good jumps."

Jump school graduation is at the fifth jump drop zone. Family and friends are invited to the drop zone and watch us make our last jump. After everyone jumps, the class is brought to attention and our jump wings are awarded right there in the field. My brother, Allan, brought my kids to observe my graduation. They got to see their mother jump out of an airplane and earn her jump wings. It was another beautiful summer day, blue skies, and sunshine. I jumped and landed without any problems. But the relief of having made it, withstanding the training and stress, and surviving my jumps finally caught up with me. Here I am, hard core Airborne Trooper, and the tears burst out of nowhere, as I kept saying to myself, "I can't believe I made it. I can't believe I made It." as I walked off the drop zone crying, tears streaming down my face.

I wish my brother could have pinned on my wings, but they told us an Airborne soldier needed to give us our wings. I would like to say I got "blood wings," where the jump sergeant slams the pins on the wings into your chest. But though I was braced for it, the jump sergeant only pushed hard enough for them to go through the fabric. I was an Airborne Paratrooper, a jump qualified member of the XVIII Airborne Corps. I was now privileged to have earned and wear jump wings and a maroon beret—the signs of an Airborne paratrooper.

I am as proud if not prouder of my graduation from jump school at 37 as I was with graduating from college at 23 with three kids. There is something about doing something physically demanding that made me feel emotionally stronger.

If I had spent a lot of time thinking about jump school and all it entailed, I may have found many reasons to talk myself out of it. But once I announced I wanted to go out loud and to other people, there was no turning back. First, I wanted to maintain my integrity and be a person of my word. Secondly, yes, I was afraid; I was scared to death. But I would have been so disappointed in myself if I did not try. And once I got there, I was too stubborn to quit. So, maybe being a little bull-headed helped. I did what was impossible and what terrified me. I earned my jump wings.

10

MOS: Military Intelligence

Something didn't fit. I needed to make a change. I loved Ft Bragg. I loved the camaraderie, the discipline and professionalism. I loved being in XVIII Airborne Corps, but as I looked around at other administrative jobs I could do, I had already done the one job that appealed to me, an Adjutant of a Battalion. I could move on to the same job in a larger unit, such as a Brigade or Corps or in a Joint assignment, but my options appeared limited. I knew I did not want to work in Administration. So, after some soul searching, I requested a branch-transfer to Military Intelligence (MI). It was a long process—more tests, letters from my commanders, a security background investigation—but finally I was accepted and ordered to Ft. Huachuca, AZ for training in the Military Intelligence Officer Advanced Course (MIOAC), and in July of 1984, I left Fort Bragg for Fort Huachuca. I traveled ahead of my kids to Ft. Huachuca. It was summer, so they stayed with my parents for a few weeks while I waited for housing.

I knew LTC Johnson, the Commander of the 58th ATC Battalion had been promoted to Colonel (O-6) and was assigned as Commander of the Air Traffic Control (ATC) Command at Ft. Huachuca, but I had not been in touch with him for a while. On my first day at Ft. Huachuca, I was driving around looking for my Bachelor Officers Quarters and ended on "Colonel's Row" where O-6 (Colonel) housing was located. I drove around the circle and, all of a sudden, I noticed COL Johnson and his wife, Pat, on the porch of one of the houses. I stopped to say hello, but before I knew it, they took my suitcase out of the car and carried it to one of their spare bedrooms. And this is where I lived until I obtained family housing and the kids joined me. I did lead a charmed life.

I loved the location of Ft. Huachuca, nestled in the mountains in Arizona, about 50 miles SE of Tucson and not far from the Mexican border. You could go out your door at any time of the day or night and hold your camera and take a picture. Between the skies and the beautiful hue of the mountains and desert, you could later enlarge any picture and frame it. It would be an array of spectacular colors. It was a different kind of beauty than I was used to—the hues of the mountains and the colors in the sky were breathtaking. The desert in the spring is magnificent to behold; cacti in bloom are incredibly beautiful. There was always a picturesque scene no matter what direction you looked. But the beauty is all from far away. Close up it is dry and prickly, oppressively dry. There is no ocean in Arizona.

I enjoyed the people attending Military Intelligence school with me, as well as the instructors and classes. As an adjutant, I was the S-1, or the administrative officer of the unit. Military Intelligence fills the role of the S-2, the person who provides the commander the tactical intelligence he needs to go into battle. This consists of analysis of the enemy, weather and terrain, evaluating the value of targets, determining what information needed to be collected, and what reconnaissance and surveillance was necessary. How well you do will determine how much the commander will rely on his S-2. For example, in Vietnam, the commander relied on the information from his S-2, who grossly underestimated the capability of the Viet Cong in the TET offensive. This resulted in the death of many soldiers. For this reason, I took my new role seriously. I found my courses fascinating. I did well even though I was a branch transfer and did not have the background my classmates had. Most of them had attended the MI Officer Basic Course and had been working a few years in MI.

At the time, the MI Advanced Course was followed by a specialty course. There are different specialties in MI: signals, imagery, human, and counterintelligence, the latter being my specialty. The Counterintelligence Officer Course was the fun stuff. A Counterintelligence Officer focuses on exploiting and neutralizing the enemy or terrorists attempting to do us harm. In this course, we learned the various means to gather intelligence and write Intelligence Information Reports (IIRs). At this time, computers were not available yet, so we had to write our IIRs on a typewriter, and they had to be perfect. We could not even use correction tape. There were many reports that had to be re-typed because of a typo at the end. We also got to go to Tucson and "tail a rabbit" (follow a person of interest) all around the city, without being detected. Afterwards, we got to be the rabbit. I loved this stuff. It was an interesting course, and fun. Yes, far more fun than AG.

The kids seemed to settle into life at Ft. Huachuca. Kelly was a junior and Amy a sophomore in the local Sierra Vista high school. Bobby was in 8th grade and went to school on Post. I remember life being easy for us. We were living in Post housing, so there were always other kids around, and the kids could walk wherever they wanted on Post. Maybe it was the relaxed atmosphere of being in school, but things were going smoothly between the kids and me. We shared quality time together. We saw the Sonora Desert Museum. We went to Tombstone and saw a re-enactment of the gunfight at the OK Corral. We went horseback riding in the hills of Ft. Huachuca. We went to Nogales, the Mexican town over the border. We visited beautiful Sedona, saw the Grand Canyon, and took a trip to San Francisco. I remember laughing a lot. Although we were only there for a year, we all made good friends. Kelly and her best friend were dating Lance and Mike, respectively. Years later Kelly would re-connect with and marry Mike.

Who knows what you will find if you are open to the possibilities each day brings. While at the Advanced Course, I met Joe, my second husband; he was in my class. There was an immediate attraction, and we dated early on. It was an especially relaxing courtship; we had time to explore the beautiful southwest, with and without the kids. We studied together and shared meals at home with the kids. I particularly loved having long conversations with Joe. Well, maybe I did most of the talking, but he listened. He always listened. At Christmastime, we traveled east to meet one another's families. It was at this time Joe broached the topic of marriage. After I got over the initial surprise, I seriously considered it.

Upon returning to Ft. Huachuca after the holidays, we talked to our assignment manager. He told us we could not apply for joint domicile (both assigned to the same location) until we were officially married, and we would have to get married by February for the military to have time to arrange joint domicile for our next assignments. So, we decided to wait, debating whether to marry in the summer before our next assignment, or wait 6 months until the Christmas holidays and then marry.

Meanwhile, our classmates were all getting their follow-on assignments. They would come to class, complaining about their options: remote locations in Korea, Alaska, and Asia. I put off calling my Assignments manager for a while, but the time finally came when I had to plan my follow-on assignment. When I called, my manager said, "Well, Carol, all I have right now is Hawaii, Belgium, and Panama." Three great choices; they all had a good US presence and a well-established base. It wasn't difficult to decide. The kids and I decided we would love living in Europe, and the Belgium assignment was with the 650th Military Intelligence Group in SHAPE. Belgium. Supreme Headquarters Allied Powers Europe is the military arm of the North Atlantic Treaty Organization (NATO). Joe's assignment was taking him to Japan.

In May, I found out I was pregnant. I was having some female medical problems and was told I could not get pregnant, but I still had to ask myself, "How could I let this happen?" I always hoped after having Kelly, Amy, and Bobby I would have more children, but the timing of this pregnancy was not good. Joe had a more difficult time with the news, not because he didn't want the baby, but because it unexpectedly put a wrench in our plans. I had faith and believed whatever happened, we would all be fine. However, even though I accepted my situation, I was terrified to go on my tour in Europe, with three teenagers, single and pregnant at 38. I was excited at the prospect of having another child, but there were still values and norms to consider. How would my new boss and co-workers regard me? How would this impact my career? How would it impact my teenage children? Neither Joe nor I considered abortion, due to our personal values and beliefs. When I told the kids, they were all excited about the prospect of a baby brother or sister. So this worry was put aside. Joe and I continued through the course with the consequences of my pregnancy weighing heavily on our minds.

During this emotional period, we received a message from the Maasches, our friends from Ft. Bragg. Amy and Bobby were visiting their father in Iowa. Kelly got the call from Marie Maasch, saying Bobby's friend, Billy, had been killed in a hit and run accident. Kelly and I sat there crying together, both devastated at the loss of someone we knew, a vibrant, happy kid, who was only 14 years old. With tears still flowing, and a lump in my throat, I called to tell Amy and Bobby. I talked to Bob before talking to the kids, because I knew they were going to need some comfort and wanted to tell him first, so he would be ready. I couldn't call Therese until the next day. When I heard the devastation and sorrow in her "hello" when she answered, I was so choked up I couldn't speak. Finally, I whispered, "Therese, this is Carol," and we sobbed together, without talking. I did not miss the connection to my own life; the blessing of another child, while here was my close friend dealing with the loss of hers.

In July, we graduated, and Joe and I went east to visit our families before leaving for our respective assignments. This time, when I told my family about the new baby, their reactions were far different than my first pregnancy. Maybe my own joy about having another baby was contagious, but they expressed joy and happiness for me as well. Joe called and suggested we visit our assignment manager together in person before we left the States. The assignment manager again repeated that the military makes every effort to provide joint domicile to military couples, but not until we were officially married. Once married, I could apply for joint domicile and join him on his tour in Japan, or he could join me on my tour in Belgium. We discussed our situation, and we both wanted this baby to be born to two parents, so despite the timing for marriage not being the best, we decided to get married before we left the States. Shortly after our civil ceremony, Joe left for Japan and the kids and I took some vacation time and went to Myrtle Beach for a week, stopping to visit the Maasch's on the way, before heading to Europe for my assignment. It was a difficult visit for all of us, but especially Bobby. Therese and Marie visited us at Myrtle Beach while we were there, but it was a somber, contemplative week for all of us.

It was time to leave for my overseas assignment and my first assignment as a Military Intelligence Officer. I was looking forward to going to Europe with the kids and anticipating the excitement of the experience. I was also happy about being married to Joe, and about having another baby.

11

SHAPE:
The European Experiences

In the words of Charles Dickens, "It was the best of times. It was the worst of times." Despite Europe being an exciting and amazing place to live, we all left a little broken. Europe itself was incredible. We have so many stories about our adventures there.

Other than Canada and Mexico, none of us had ever been out of the country. We had no idea what to expect. Luckily when a military member is assigned to a new base, a sponsor is designated to assist with in-processing and directions around the new location. This is especially helpful in a foreign country. My sponsor met us at the airport in Belgium and took us to our hotel in Mons, Belgium.

I found out at my in-processing I would be put on a long waiting list for Post family housing; the wait could take 18 months. So, we went house hunting in Mons. My sponsor, who spoke a little French, came with us. We had the address to a potential house, and upon arrival, knocked on the door, and proceeded to enter. The family was gathered around the table eating a meal, and they strangely looked at us when we came in. I left my sponsor talking to the house owners and getting the details of when the house was available and the rental cost. In the meantime, the kids and I explored, going from room to room, checking out the closets and the layout, when all of a sudden, my sponsor said, "Carol, we have to leave." Well, as in the States, we have avenues and roads and streets, all with the same name, so did Mons, Belgium. We were at the wrong address, on an avenue when we should have been on a street. I picture this family, still talking about the weird Americans who invaded their privacy, walked into their home, and looked through their closets.

We found a row house in Mons, the city where Supreme Headquarters Allied Powers Europe (SHAPE) was located. It was a grand old house with 18-foot ceilings on the first floor and cut-glass panels in the doors between the living room and dining room and kitchen. You ascended one flight to the bathroom, and another flight to two bedrooms (mine and Bobby's), followed by two more flights to two more bedrooms (Kelly and Amy's), and a couple more flights to the attic. Outside in the backyard was a beautiful rose garden. We were within walking distance of Mons and about a 10-minute drive to SHAPE. The house was awesome, and we were thrilled to find it. It was authentically European.

Shortly after arriving at SHAPE, I confided to my sponsor I was married and was going to request joint domicile. I asked for her opinion on who would be the best person to approach with this news. She suggested the Deputy Commander. Based on her input I went to the Deputy and informed him I was married, and I would be requesting joint domicile with my husband, who was stationed in Japan. He quickly responded, telling me because I traveled with dependents, I had a two-year obligation. My husband only had a one-year obligation since he traveled solo. Now we had new decisions to make about who goes where and when. Deciding not to wait two years for us to join him, my husband impulsively requested joint domicile to SHAPE. He was losing a prime, covert intelligence assignment, highly competitive, and one he had long worked towards, to join us in Europe. This troubled me, even though I was happy he was coming. We could make the extra year apart work for us. We could still get together for vacations and holidays. However, he decided and moved towards leaving his assignment in Japan.

My job at the 650th MI Group was great. First, I was the Assistant S-2 (Intel Staff Officer), and I had to do threat reports for the Supreme Allied Commander, Europe (SACEUR) if he was traveling. This was not a good time in Europe; many terrorist groups were active. The Red Army Faction (RAF) was a West German, far-left organization and was considered a terrorist group. The previous SACEUR, Alexander Haig, escaped death when the RAF bombed his car. Security was on high alert. I also had the chance to interact with Intel officers from other countries in meetings on post. And our unit specifically had a counterpart German Intelligence Group we met with semiannually, first at their site and subsequently at ours. We had the opportunity to fire each other's weapons and end the day with amazing food and lots of beer.

One of my work responsibilities was to go to Bonn, Germany and meet with the Intelligence Officers there. I arrived, met my counterpart, and proceeded to give him the briefing I had put together. By this time, my fourth pregnancy was obvious. I was only 5 minutes into my briefing when he stopped me, "Would you like to sit? Are you comfortable? Can I get you anything?" I assured him I was fine and continued. About a half hour into it, he stopped me again. "Are you sure you are, okay? Wouldn't you like to sit?" I assured him I was still running three times a week and was fine, but he was annoying me. I appreciated his concern, but I was used to ignoring my pregnancy and concentrating on doing my job. I was uncomfortable. I was not some frail little thing needing to spend nine months in bed if I was pregnant. However, after this, I noticed I did not see a lot of pregnant women walking around Belgium or Germany. Maybe they stayed indoors? Luckily, my pregnancies were easy, and I continued to run and walk through my whole pregnancy. I also worked until delivery.

The kids and I all seemed to settle into our own routines. During my time at SHAPE, I made many friends at church, and they were a great support during this time of pregnancy, marriage, and settling into our new home. I also taught high school religious education and my children as well as many of their friends were in my class. Kelly, Amy, and Bobby were all in high school at the time. They were also all involved in high school activities: football, basketball, track, wrestling, and cheerleading, as well as serving in leadership positions on the student council. They immersed themselves in all the experiences Europe had to offer. They went on location to study famous battles or see famous castles; they went to London to see Shakespeare or to Paris to study Hemingway, checking out all his favorite meeting places. They visited museums and art galleries. It was a small school, and between the three of them, they quickly knew everybody in the school.

Joe tried to strategically schedule a trip in December 1985 to coincide with the birth of our child. But, since he wouldn't be there to go through childbirth classes with me, Kelly accompanied me. Luckily, my husband made it there in time for the delivery, but I still relied on Kelly to coach me through delivery. When I went into labor, I called the school, requesting Kelly to come to the hospital. The high school office obliged. On her way out of school, Kelly stopped by Amy and Bobby's classes and declared, "Mom's in labor." I didn't deliver until after four in the afternoon. Later, I found out there were about 20 high school kids in the waiting room, keeping my kids company while waiting for the new arrival. When it was time for the birth, Amy and Bobby joined Kelly in the delivery room to witness Joey's birth. They didn't have to stay, but I was glad they did, and I hope the miracle of birth left an impression on them.

Joey was born days before the Christmas holidays. I had agreed earlier for the kids to have a party at the house. As it turned out, their Christmas party was the same day I returned from the hospital with their new brother. The whole SHAPE High School was invited. So, Joey was introduced early to the sounds of lots of people around him. I was also surprised and delighted at how many of these high school kids were interested and wanted to see the baby.

My husband, Joe, was able to stay for almost a month on leave and take advantage of the time to bond with his son. No child could have as many pictures taken as Joey did. My parents came at the same time to visit and meet their new grandchild. While they were there, I went for my four-week check-up. The doctor became cautiously alarmed when he saw a huge growth manifesting itself in the short amount of time between delivery and my follow-on check-up. He immediately scheduled a biopsy and was talking about the possibility of a medevac back to a hospital in the States. I was terrified. Joe was scheduled to return to Japan the day before my surgery, and I was hurt and shocked he did not request an extension. However, my parents were there to help with the kids, so I had support around me. As it turned out, the tumor was benign, and they removed it. However, the doctor had to pack me with gauze to control the bleeding. When I awoke from surgery, my father was there. I remember being in pain from the surgery, uncomfortable with the packing, and worried about my milk drying out for the baby I was nursing. There were a myriad of emotions at work as well, and I incessantly sobbed to my father, who sat there, clearly frustrated and helpless in the presence of his crying daughter. I remember his love and tenderness, while trying to find some way to comfort me. He stayed with me all night and I remember waking to his tired and concerned eyes. I experienced this man's tenderness and love, a fond memory tucked away in my heart.

The military gave me three weeks' maternity leave but extended it another week after my surgery. I found an amazing young British woman, married to a British officer, to watch Joey when I returned to work. Ironically, she had a little boy born within days of Joey. Nevertheless, it was heart-wrenching to leave Joey and go to work. I expected he would cry when I left but found out from the nanny, he cried all day long. And he cried the next day and the next day. In fact, it took almost two weeks for him to settle into the new arrangement. The older children were great with the baby. There was no shortage of help, at least until the novelty wore off, but still they were enamored with him. They all bonded when, as a baby, Joey would accompany me to his older sibling's sporting and school events.

Despite outward appearances, Kelly was having a difficult time during the first year at SHAPE. Prior to this assignment, the Army moved us three times: this impacted all the kids, but Kelly had the most difficult time. She had been in high school at Fayetteville (Ft. Bragg) for two years followed by high school in Arizona for one year. This was her third high school in four years. Only a month after we arrived, she was elected a class officer and was nominated to Homecoming Court. On the outside, she had it all together, but on the inside, she was in emotional turmoil; she had a suicide attempt. I'm embarrassed to say Amy pointed it out to me. I was devastated. How could I miss this? How could I not see she didn't want to live anymore? What if she succeeded? What if my beautiful daughter died? I tried to excuse myself by saying I was extremely busy with my husband in Japan, and a new baby and working full time and raising three teenagers in a foreign country, but this doesn't excuse me from not knowing what Kelly was going through. I immediately got her into counseling. She was initially so angry, saying I was pawning her off on someone else, because I didn't want to deal with her. The reality was I already failed at being able to help her, or she would not have attempted suicide. She later admitted the counselor was the best thing that ever happened to her.

A couple months after Joey was born, Joe was able to obtain Joint Domicile with me in Belgium. We settled into married life together. It was an adjustment for both of us. I had designed a schedule for the kids and me which worked. Now we all had to adjust to accommodate someone else in our schedule. This was difficult for Joe, as he was disappointed about the job he lost and hated his new job with the 650th MI Group. We also disagreed on having a religious wedding ceremony. He did not want to be married in the church until we were on more solid ground. I believed a religious ceremony would strengthen our bond. Nonetheless, we finally decided to go to Buffalo the next summer and have a religious ceremony and a small reception for our relatives and friends. Kelly and Amy were my maids of honor, and Joe's brother Jay was his best man. Joe admitted afterwards he was glad we did it; it was a beautiful event.

Our life at SHAPE was busy, but we still managed to have a social life. We would sometimes have friends over for dinner, and the older kids loved getting Joey to perform. One night Kelly, Amy, and Bobby were eating with some teens in the other room with Joey. All of a sudden, I heard this loud laughter. Upon checking it out, I saw Joey was mimicking what they were doing. They were rubbing the top of their heads, grasping their faces. However, we had spaghetti for dinner and Joey was eating with his hands, and now spaghetti was spread all over his head and face. The older kids were laughing hysterically.

Kelly was finishing her senior year of high school, and she was dating the valedictorian of the class. He was a quiet, religious guy who had been accepted at all three military academies and chose to go to the Air Force Academy. Additionally, she always had male friends who befriended the rest of our family as well. She was respected and admired by her classmates and admired by her brother and sister. She was my right arm. She finished her senior year, involved in school and social activities, was elected Prom Queen, and was leaving for college in the fall.

When we were back in Buffalo for the church wedding

ceremony, I was able to take Kelly to Syracuse University and help get her settled in. This was a difficult transition for all of us. I was single for 10 years before marrying Joe. Kelly had become the "heart" of the family. She was everyone's confidant, and she was the peacemaker. I'm not sure if the roles were dumped on her or if she assumed them. Since I was the sole breadwinner, she saw a hole in the family and filled it. This was a lot of responsibility for a young girl. It is not surprising she had been in such emotional turmoil. When she left for school, we all experienced her absence, and she had an equally difficult time at school, on her own. She was an ocean away from all of us. She would call and be so homesick, she would break down in tears. I would try to comfort her and tell her it would get better. But I would hang up and cry. If only she wasn't so far away. Someone recently inquired, "Why didn't she go to school in Europe for a couple years?" This never even entered my mind. Looking back, it would have been a great solution. We could have seen her more regularly, and she was unquestionably astute at learning languages and would have done extremely well. Regrettably, we weren't aware and didn't consider other options.

Soon after Joe joined us, I became pregnant again but this time the pregnancy was planned. There was a 14 to 16-year age difference between Joey and his older siblings, and we wanted him to have a sibling closer to his own age. When I got pregnant again, I remember calling to share the news with Kelly, and heard her yell to the dorm, "My mom is pregnant."

One of the family benefits of the military is housing, and we finally came to the top of the list for post housing. We qualified for a 5-bedroom house. It was all on one floor, with 3 bathrooms and 5 bedrooms all off the hallway leading from the kitchen/living area. It looked like a hotel corridor. Our neighbors on one side were German, with two boys about a year older than Joey. There were Brits on the other side, with a little boy Joe's age, and there was a Scandinavian couple across the street with a couple boys older than Joey. All these kids spoke different languages, yet they all played together outside, speaking the common language of childhood. These kids could give lessons to adults having important meetings on how to get along with each other.

Amy was now in her senior year. She was born less than a year after Kelly, who was the first baby in the family in years. As a baby, Amy tended to be fussy and cried a lot, at a time when Kelly was entertaining the family with all her new accomplishments. But despite being sidelined initially, as Amy grew older, she learned to carve her own niche. She was sweet and loving and unspoiled. Our relatives enjoyed her shyness, and she was a friend to her cousins who loved her playfulness. She had her own hurdles to overcome. In one year, she was fitted with braces and had to wear glasses. She was a late bloomer as her mother was, which is excruciating for a teenager. But like the ugly duckling, in her sophomore year, her braces came off, and she was able to get contacts. Her femininity blossomed. She was beautiful and radiated the joy of life. She was popular and always had friends who were dedicated and loyal.

In the summer of 1987, Amy graduated from high school after a tumultuous end to her senior year. As sweet and sensitive as she was, she was the middle child and often got lost in family commotion. All of us missed Kelly in our own ways, but it was especially difficult for Amy. Amy always had good friends, but she also had a special bond with her sister. Kelly was popular, which came with its own problems, and Amy grew up in her shadow. Here at SHAPE, Amy was finding her own identity. She played basketball and ran track. She was an officer on the student council. She had many friends. And she found out she was attractive to boys. She was also learning some life lessons the hard way. Days before graduation, she got in trouble at school and, as a result, she was restricted from school activities. I had meetings with school officials and wrote a letter regarding the lack of ethics and integrity of one of the teachers. The principal finally agreed to let her participate in graduation events. Kelly had returned to Belgium for the summer, and we all went to Amy's Baccalaureate. Baccalaureate was a non-denominational graduation event held at the Chapel. There was a mother (the mom of one of Amy's former boyfriends) who oversaw Baccalaureate. She did not like Amy and took it upon herself to restrict Amy from participating in the event, saying it was a school activity, not a graduation activity. Essentially, she was saying Amy could not sit with her class for the ceremony, her name was stricken from the roles, and she was never mentioned as a class officer. I begged and pleaded with her, but she would not budge. I still have resentment and a few choice names for this woman. The principal was unavailable to clarify the matter. So, our whole family sat off to the side, with Kelly, Amy, and me all sobbing through the ceremony. After it was over, we immediately returned home. Within minutes, cars were parking in front of our house. All of Amy's friends and their families were stopping by to support and comfort Amy. It was such a heart-wrenching act of love.

Shortly after Amy's graduation, I delivered Franky, a few weeks earlier than anticipated. At a routine doctor's appointment, the doctor told me the baby was a "footling breech": the baby was positioned with one leg pushing into the birth canal. The doctor admitted me to the hospital right away and scheduled a Cesarean section delivery the next morning. I came home a couple days later and was not prepared for the prolonged recovery from a C-Section. It was summer and the kids were out of school, so I had a lot of help with now two babies, one 18 months old and one a newborn.

After much soul-searching with Joe, following Frank's birth in the fall of 1987, I separated from active duty. Yes, this was what I was meant to do, but my family needed me more right now. Amy left to attend University of Rochester, Joe was working at the 650th MI Group as well, and I now had two babies to care for, as well as our home and my job. I was juggling all the balls, but Joe worked long hours and I could support him and his career better, and ease the stress at home, if I was a stay-at-home mom. I understood I would not be able to come back on active duty, but my role at home was more important. Joe supported this decision. I was released from active duty. At the time, I did not agonize about this decision and the impact on my military career. Did I make the right decision?

I wanted to continue in the Army as a reservist, so I found an Individual Mobilization Augmentee (IMA) position with an Army Intelligence Agency in Belgium. As an IMA, I did not have to attend monthly drills, but was required to work for two weeks a year with my assigned unit.

Joe was never comfortable keeping the boys by himself, maybe because I was nursing Franky, or he was uneasy with babies. So, when Bobby had a sporting event, I packed the diaper bags, suitcases, and the two babies and headed off to the SHAPE gym or a town in Germany or wherever the event was taking place. If we took a train, this entailed loading the boys and all our gear onto the platform, on and off the train, and to the sporting event. But once there, I always had the support of other families.

Frank was a loving, extremely tactile baby—he loved to touch things: the texture of fabrics, the softness of my skin next to him, he touched everything. He never outgrew this; even as a teen he would only wear clothes made from certain fabrics. People would stop me and tell me what a beautiful baby he was. He was always actively engaging with other people and would make friends with anyone who talked to him. He adored his older brothers, Joey as well as Bobby. And he was easygoing, more so than his brother Joe, who even as a toddler took everything so seriously, concentrating on every task he did. Joey would watch Bobby wrestle and come home and perform the same moves on his stuffed animals. At two years old, he wanted us to take the training wheels off his bike and was riding a two-wheeled bike around the circle where we lived.

One year at Christmas we all went to a military resort in Garmisch, Germany, for the holidays. The girls were home, Bobby had not yet graduated, and Joey and Franky were two years and six months respectively. We all got to ski the German Alps. It was a grand location in the mountains. We drove on the mountain as far as we could, took a trolley car to the lodge, and rode ski lifts to the slopes. The views were awesome. From the top of the mountain, Zugspitze, all you could see, as far as you looked, were mountains of snow. It looked like we were on top of mounds of clouds. We could see Austria and Switzerland from there. I requested everyone take a day to watch the boys, so I would be able to enjoy our vacation as well. Joe and I took a day and went to Oberammergau. It was quaint and beautiful. We also took a day and went skiing, with Joey. We put him on skis, and he did better than I did. Despite my age, I had never skied before. There were a lot of other families from SHAPE at Garmisch, and we all had friends to celebrate New Year's Eve. This was a great vacation for all of us.

Bobby was having a great year. He played football and wrestled. He was second in his weight class in the European championship. And he was an easy child to raise. He always admitted his wrongdoings and accepted the consequences without giving excuses. I remember once calling the school to leave him a message and I was told he was at home, sick for the day. I responded, "Well, this is his mother and I guarantee he is not home sick, and I believe you have a truant student." My easy-to-raise son was challenging the system and committing unacceptable high school pranks, but still accepted the consequences of his actions: detention for skipping school and his mom ratting him out.

Joe and I recognized we had problems, and we were work-ing on our marriage; we were in counseling. In January the counselor told us we had a breakthrough and were at a point he was hopeful we would make it. It was the first time he was optimistic. Weeks later, Joe announced he received orders for an unaccompanied tour in Korea. It seems one night when he was particularly disheartened by our marriage, he went to work and requested this unaccompanied tour. When it came through, I tried to be hopeful, this might be a good opportu-nity for us to use this time to bond in a different way through letters. I was convinced we could make it work for us.

In June 1989, Bobby graduated from high school. His fa-ther came to Belgium to be with him for this event. I remem-ber watching the two of them walk; same build, same gait, each with their right hand in their right pocket. Bobby had not lived with Bob since he was five. How could he have learned so many of his mannerisms? I found this fascinating.

Joe was finishing his assignment at SHAPE in July. We had agreed I would return to Buffalo with the boys, to be near family while he was gone. A few weeks prior to leaving, Joe announced he did not plan to return to me after Korea. I was devastated. I did not see this coming. I agreed with our coun-selor we were making progress. In retrospect, I did not make coming into a premade family with three teenagers easy on Joe. Prior to meeting him, I had been a single parent and was used to making all decisions. I didn't remember to ask for his input. But for whatever his own reasons, he wanted a divorce. Was our marriage a mistake? We entered it with love. We had two children born out of love. Although what followed was difficult and emotional, I will never see it as a mistake, but part of my life's journey.

As I look back on our European experience, it was amazing. We had not one but two additions to our family. Each of us had amazing experiences we will never forget. But in the midst of all these exciting adventures, we each had our own diffi-culties and life challenges to deal with. Bobby broke his arm during a wrestling match. This break could be fixed. Amy had to experience and deal with the painful, unfair consequences of life. Kelly almost had a lethal tragedy. Joey and Franky were separated from their father. My marriage failed, and I was no longer on active duty. But we had the strength and comfort of each other. We would overcome our challenges.

12

Survival: Life After Active Duty

The next seven years were all about surviving and moving on after active duty. Upon arrival in Buffalo, I searched for full time work and a new reserve position. The closest MI assignment was an Individual Mobilization Augmentation (IMA) position with the Intelligence Threat Analysis Center (ITAC) in Washington, DC. So, I attended annual training in DC for two weeks every year, working as an Intel Analyst at the Intelligence Threat and Analysis Center, and later the National Ground and Intelligence Center in Charlottesville, VA.

The next thing on my agenda, after moving to Buffalo, was to find our own place. We were thrilled to find a small house to rent and enjoyed our time there. I was still holding out hope that Joe and I could reconcile. After we left Belgium, he had to go to school for three months before heading for Korea. I was hoping during this time, he would discover how much he missed the kids and me and we could move forward together. He came to visit the boys after completion of his schooling, before heading to Korea. I was excited and hopeful. He played with the boys, and I remember looking at him, "I positively love this man." I put the kids to bed and was looking forward to an evening of connection and resolve. But when I returned after putting Joey and Franky to sleep, Joe said, "I've got a separation agreement here I would like you to sign; in a year we can file for a no-fault divorce." This was not exactly the romantic evening I had planned. I was taken aback and blindsided, although this was my own optimism; he never truly gave me any cause for hope. He obviously had been thinking about this for a while, but I had not. I needed more time before I was ready to sign the papers. He left and shortly after he arrived in Korea, he filed for divorce.

Because two weeks a year did not give me enough points to count as a valid year toward retirement, I quickly looked for some other military assignment to provide me enough points for a qualifying year and to supplement my income. My Personnel Manager found me a slot with the Directorate of Evaluation and Standardization (DOES) at Ft. Devens, MA for four months, from mid-May and to mid-September. This job was under the title of Active Duty, Special Work (ADSW) so I was essentially on active duty for four months a year. This provided the barest minimum I needed to stay home with the boys for the remainder of the year. Joey and Franky were only toddlers, not yet in school. I also did some substitute teaching and cleaned houses to augment my income.

Every summer during this time, Joey, Frank, and I would head out to Ft. Devens, MA for my ADSW tour. Joe had resigned his commission in 1991 after his tour in Korea and our divorce became final. Because at the time he had no job and his only income was the annuity the Army gave him when he resigned, the court awarded me $2600 a year in child support for Joey and Franky. When I tried to take him to court for more, I found he was immune from the US court system, since he had moved to the Philippines. Not much had changed in the court's view of the financial burden for single moms since my earlier experience in the 1970s.

My niece, Wendy, came with me for the summer to babysit and earn some money for school clothes. We still laugh when we get together about all the fun times we had during those summers. Like the time a couple from church came and stayed with us. We all woke in the middle of the night to a snore sounding like a freight train coming through the room. I had to stop Wendy from heading towards the man with a pillow to stop the noise.

The summers were great for all of us. I would come home at lunchtime and take Wendy and my boys to the beach, which was right on base. They would spend the afternoon there, and I would get them after work. In the evening we would go to the movies or local small amusement parks. On weekends, we would go to Boston and see the sites, go on whale watches, see military reenactments, and generally enjoy the summer in the Boston area. I remember especially the 4th of July celebration at the Hatch Shell. We went to Boston for the festivities and the crowd was growing. I noticed a seating area was roped off in front of the stage and I went to the guard, "Why are you letting some people in and others are turned away?" He answered they were letting in the handicapped and military. At which point I immediately pulled out my military ID, and he lifted the rope and let the four of us in for seating. We had front row seats to the Boston Pops and the fireworks. It was great.

Another benefit of my tour at Ft. Devens was the boys were able to see their paternal aunts and uncles, who were in the New England area, and their grandparents, who were in Albany. They came to visit us, and we went to see them. They remain an active part of the boys' lives to this day.

In the army, once a year (or sooner depending on circumstances) I got an Officer's Evaluation Report (OER). This was my report card. This is how I was evaluated against my peers on promotion boards and command boards. The importance of a good evaluation cannot be overestimated, since if I was passed over for promotion two times, I would be released from active duty. Once I learned the importance of these evaluations, I decided to go to my boss halfway through my rating period and ask him/her if he had to rate me, how would I be rated? I reasoned that if there were things he or she was not pleased with, I would have enough time to fix it before my official evaluation. This worked well for me and helped me verify the level of my performance throughout the rating period, gave me time to fine tune and discuss with my rater how I could improve my performance.

One of the joys of being back in Buffalo was I was able to spend time with my friend, Jacqie. She had gone through a divorce and remarried and had a little girl between the ages of Joe and Frank. It was great having a friend who was having similar experiences who could commiserate with me. Line dancing was the craze, and we both took on this new pursuit, providing many Friday nights of fun. But during those years, Jacqie was diagnosed with breast cancer and started treatments. I was glad I was there for her during those times, but it was particularly difficult for me because I had already seen a childhood friend as well as my neighbor, young women in their 30s, die of breast cancer. But Jacqie had an amazing constitution and took many things into her own hands, including researching and learning about new treatments and finding a doctor who would work with her. She dealt with her treatments with determination and an attitude of "let's get this done and on to healthier living."

With only two weeks annual training and four months active duty every year, I had time to focus on my family. Also, I was active in my church and was again teaching religious education to high school students. I was able to have family over for birthday parties and holidays, especially Christmas. We were all thrilled to share these events with extended family, after being stationed out of the area for so many years.

One year, for Franky's fourth birthday, I had some family and friends over for a party. Some of the boys' friends from the neighborhood were there, and the kids were all playing while the adults were visiting with each other. Joe called to wish Franky a Happy Birthday. When he was done talking to

Franky, Joe wanted to talk to Joey.

Franky told Joey, "Daddy wants to talk to you." In the middle of games with his friends, Joey said, "I'll talk to him later. I'm playing right now."

"Daddy, Joey doesn't want to talk now."

Joe (yelling loudly): "You tell him he damn well better talk to me. I am his father. Tell him to come to the phone, NOW."

Franky (crying and upset): "Joey, you have to talk to him now."

I grabbed the phone. "Joe, we are in the middle of Franky's party. I have a house full of company. We will call you back later when everybody leaves." To which he responded, "You tell him if he won't talk to me now, I will never talk to him again." and he hung up.

Joe kept his word until he tragically ended his life 30 years later in 2020. He never talked to Joey, sent presents, or saw him again. Joey was five and a half years old. Later, Franky connected and communicated with his father, but the next time Joey (at age 34) saw his father was at his funeral.

In August 1991, my daughter Amy married Mike, a great guy she had met at the University of Rochester. One day, as they were planning their wedding, Amy and Mike came to me requesting some support. Traditionally, the groom's parents covered the drinks at the wedding. Mike's parents decided they did not want to. I get it: an open bar can mean some people will use it as an excuse to drink to excess and get drunk. They did not want to support this. However, my family has this pride about providing food and drink for anyone attending a party we are hosting. If my father saw any of his relatives or friends paying for their own drink, he would be at the bar, paying for drinks all night. I shared this viewpoint, so I agreed to cover an open bar for their wedding. Amy and Mike covered a large part of their wedding expenses, but I was willing to help as much as I could. I wrote to Amy's father, Bob, to ask for some help for the wedding. He lamented, "Sorry, no I can't. I recently remarried and have a family to support and am starting my own business. It's an extremely bad time."

Ft. Devens came out on the Base Realignment and Closure (BRAC) list in 1992. The base was closing, and I would no longer be working there during the summer. By this time the boys were in school. Even though I was able to make some extra money during this time, substitute teaching and cleaning houses, it wasn't enough. Finally, I found a full-time job at a Social Service Agency servicing the off-reservation Native Americans in Buffalo. I was thankful for the job, and had some remarkable experiences, but did not see myself in this position long term.

Less than two years after Amy's wedding, in July 1993, Kelly married another Mike, who she had met when I was stationed at Ft. Huachuca in 1984-85. I was so happy for my daughters—they were making careful, wise choices for men to share their lives with. Kelly and I were talking about her wedding plans one day and she looked at me. "So, what is it like for me to be getting married and not your little girl anymore? I will have a husband who will be the primary person in my life." I considered this. She obviously saw this as part of her growing up process, her disconnecting from me. However, when she left home and went away to school was the time I experienced the separation and loss of her moving on. This was the transition for me. I was fascinated. She had been on her own for seven years. What did this mean for her? Did she need more nurturing and involvement from me these last few years? I am still not sure what to make of it. It was another missed opportunity for a deeper conversation.

In early December 1994, my assignment manager called to inquire if I would be interested in a three-month position at the Intelligence School at Fort Huachuca. Picture this: winter in Buffalo, NY, freezing cold and miserable, boots, jackets, gloves all the time, feet, not inches, of snow and ice and he wanted to know if I was interested in going to sunny, warm Arizona for three months? Honestly? I immediately gave him a positive response. As luck would have it, my initial 90-day tour turned into a year and a half in sunny, warm Arizona.

The kids enjoyed school in Arizona as well. They went to school on post, so I was always close by if they needed anything. I remember a parent teacher's conference with one of Frank's teachers. Her description of Frank's personality is spot on to this day. After talking about what a caring and friendly boy he was, she stopped and smiled. "You know, while everyone else is happily driving in one direction, Frank will always be driving the opposite way, smiling and waving happily to everyone as he passes." Early in his life, Frank seemed to be carving out his own way.

Joe, on the other hand, always gravitated toward sports. And he was good. He was playing Pop Warner football in Buffalo before we left. When we were still in Arizona the next summer, his coach called and offered to let Joe come and live with him so he could play football in the fall. I still smile when I remember this. Did he realistically believe this was an option? Maybe if he offered a car and a good salary, I would consider letting Joe move back to Buffalo for his peewee football career. In Arizona, he switched to baseball and his team went on to state finals towards the Little League World Series.

We enjoyed many activities, on our own and with other families. Revisiting some of the same places I went to with Kelly, Amy, and Bobby 10 years earlier, we went to Tombstone and witnessed the re-enactment of the gunfight at the OK Corral. We went horseback riding in the Huachuca mountains. We went to Sedona to see the beautiful rock formations and the Sonora Desert Museum to learn about some plants and animals of the desert. We enjoyed a progressive Thanksgiving dinner with friends starting at one house for appetizers at 10 a.m., and eight houses later we finished with desserts at 9 p.m.

We rented a great house in Sierra Vista with a built-in swimming pool, and pool maintenance came with the rent. On Easter, we hosted an Easter Sunday brunch. I invited some of the kids' friends and their families, and some of my coworkers and friends. They came at about 11 and we ate; the kids were playing in the pool and having a great time and the adults were enjoying some drinks and talking and relaxing. At 6 p.m., everyone was still there, so we brought out the leftovers, added some hamburgers and everyone stayed till almost 10pm. It was an outstanding time for all of us.

One day Amy called and told me she was pregnant. I was elated. She was coming for a visit and while she was visiting, I was able to call some of my friends together and we threw her a baby shower. It was great to be so far away from where she was living and still be able to enjoy and share this special time in her life.

During this time, I received a call from Bobby, who was living in my apartment back in Buffalo. He told me he had some news and advised me to sit. Bobby was one of those people everyone liked. He's got a great wit and is knowledgeable and loyal to his family and friends alike. His uncles and grandfather were his male role models, and they impacted his personality. They gave him his sense of masculinity. This resulted in a sense of determination throughout his life. Despite his 5-foot, 8 inch, 98 pound build, he tried out and made the high school football team, as well as the wrestling team. His two older sisters rounded out his personality by teaching him everything he needed to know about girls. He became adept at treating girls special. In high school, he worked for one of my co-workers, weeding her yard, so he could make enough money to make an impact and impress his prom date. Bobby made some close friendships during his high school years and is in touch with many of them to this day. There were three friends in particular he was close to, and they and Bobby (all sons of military members) declared "No way am I joining the military; it is not for me." So, when Bobby called and blurted out, "I enlisted in the Army," I was utterly taken by surprise. Bobby was the last holdout, enlisting in the Army, as did his friends, Guy, and Adam. Sean went to ROTC and became a Navy officer. "OMG, this is great, but why didn't you call me earlier? Maybe I could have helped." But he made the decision and went for it. Since his high school graduation, he had a couple jump-starts, but still had not found his career path. I admit I was proud of him, and I was hopeful this would be a satisfying career for him.

During my time at Ft. Huachuca, my rater and senior rater suggested I apply for the AGR (Active Guard/Reserve) program, wherein I could come back into the Army full time. So, I applied. I found out in February 1996 I was high on the order of merit list, but they were not considering majors, because they could hire two captains for the cost of one major. Learning from earlier experiences, I again wrote a letter and pleaded my case. In May, I got a call. I was selected for the AGR program, and my first assignment would be at the Army Reserve Readiness Training Center (ARRTC) as a Training Instructor. I was going to teach the Instructor Training Course (ITC) to potential instructors. The ARRTC was in Sparta, WI, so I went back to Buffalo, packed my apartment, and Joe, Frank, and I headed for Wisconsin, and in August 1996, I was back on Active Duty.

Some might be skeptical regarding the power of prayer; however, there are a lot of paths this tour in Arizona could have taken, with a lot of different outcomes. As on all military bases, there was a chapel on base and I was able to attend daily services, when possible. This was always a source of strength for me. So ever diligent in my prayer for guidance, I have no doubt God was watching over the kids and me and this path was the one I was meant to be on. We might have missed so many great opportunities. Despite all my starts and stops in the army, I was on active duty again. This time there was no doubt in my mind this was my calling. This was my life's work and this time I would be here for the rest of my career. I was coming back to where I was meant to be all along.

13

Life: Beginnings and Endings

I was back on active duty in the Army. This new assignment grounded me in my career, stabilized my financial well-being, and was a period of acceptance in my family. I viewed the assignment as a low-visibility job keeping me under the radar of the Commander, who rated me. However, halfway through my first year at the ARRTC, I went to the Commander to ask him if he was satisfied with my performance and if he had any recommendations on how I could improve. He looked at me almost mischievously, "Carol, don't worry about anything, the walls have ears, and I am perfectly aware of the work you do." This sounded good to me.

I had the finances for the first time in my life to purchase a home in Sparta, Wisconsin. I learned a valuable lesson from the layout of our house. The house was a ranch-style home with three bedrooms on the main floor. In addition, it had a semi-finished basement, with two more bedrooms. I finished off the basement. I mean, I personally finished off the dry-walling of the ceiling and walls in the basement. I saw my father and brothers build their own homes, and they made it look so easy, so I reasoned "of course I can do this." If I ever talk about taking a project like this on again, please, just shoot me. It was way more work than I had anticipated. After the job was finished, the two boys moved into the bedrooms downstairs.

There was also an eating area and a television and sitting area in the basement. The boys quickly established their domain. When we had family movie night, I would join them. Otherwise, they would watch their shows, and I would watch mine upstairs. I learned when kids have their own space for TV and for games, I could go many hours without ever interfacing with them. I missed their presence, if not their interactions.

Sparta was a beautiful midwestern town. We lived about a mile out of town. The local golf course offered kids under 16 a deal: for $25 for the summer, they could golf as often as they wanted. I got both the boys golf lessons, and they could ride their bikes to the golf course. Most of their friends also took advantage of the offer, so almost every day they would play golf. Joe would sometimes play three rounds a day, but at least two. In the winter, Saturday mornings were family deals at the small hill on post, which offered downhill skiing. Although it wasn't the Alps, it offered us some winter fun and exercise. We all looked forward to those Saturday mornings skiing with neighbors and friends.

Shortly after arriving in Wisconsin, my best friend, Jacqie called to talk to me about driving to Wisconsin to see us. Jacqie was going through remission with her breast cancer. I was excited to have time to visit with her. One night while she was visiting, we went out to a local bar. I had not dated since I was married to Joe and was at a time in my life when my focus was on raising Joe and Frank and working on my career. We were sitting at the bar and having a great time having some great conversations, when Jacqie observed, "Carol, one guy over there is staring at you." I turned and looked at the guy sitting at the other end and turned, "Jacqie, he doesn't have any teeth!" to which she teased, "Picky, Picky, Picky." I still laugh about this.

The boys and I were involved with other families, neighbors, and church. I enrolled the boys in the small Catholic school. With all the moving my children had to do, it was my priority in their early years for them to attend school where they felt safe and secure. The private school offered a more nurturing environment as well as teachers who focused on their individual needs. For example, Joe's teacher recognized he was bored, so the teacher worked out an accelerated program for Joe in some of his classes. One of Frank's teachers was concerned about some stories Frank had written. She was worried he was going through a disturbing and troubling time. I took this seriously and decided to take both boys for some counseling. The counselor gave us some tools for talking to one another and taught the boys there was always some place to go to get help when overwhelmed. This helped us learn to live our lives more connected and related to each other in more effective ways.

Towards the end of my first year, the Commandant (COL Jon Robinett) called me in to tell me he was going to reorganize the structure and leadership of the ARRTC. His plan was to take one of the two O-5 engineering positions and make it an O-5 Deputy Commandant slot. He sought my opinion, this was interesting. Why me? Why did he care what I thought? So, I inquired why he was re-structuring, and he told me the organization was growing. He was the immediate supervisor and rater for all the civilians and field grade officers. He was dealing with other agencies and supporting the needs of the Army for readiness. He needed a Deputy to share these responsibilities. This made sense. But he told me he wanted me to fill the Deputy position. I was shocked. I did not see this coming. This was a real compliment. I considered it for a nano-second and quickly accepted. So, we scheduled regular meetings to review some of the issues he was dealing with, introducing me to others around the Post and filling me in on his expectations for a deputy. During one of these meetings, the Major, who was in the O-5 slot converting to the Deputy position, came in to talk to the Commandant. He proceeded to tell the Commandant why he would be a better choice than me for the Deputy slot. I was listening to him, and he made some good points, even though I did not like him personally. He was kind of arrogant. The Commandant looked at him directly. "I agree with you, the best, most qualified person should be selected for this position. I looked at all the criteria you mentioned, and I did select the most qualified person for the job." COL Robinette believed in me. Yes, I may have gloated a little bit. This other major was much smarter than I was, but I had better people skills. I learned another lesson in leadership. It's important to know your job, but sometimes intelligence is not enough; it's also necessary to work effectively with people.

So, I moved into an office in the Command Group and became the Deputy. I embraced this position and loved working with COL Robinett. He was amazing. I was learning so much from him about leadership. As the Deputy Commandant, I assisted the Commander in all aspects of running the ARRTC and took command in his absence. I mentored, coached, and guided the professional development of civilians and military personnel within the Command. I resolved personnel issues and conflicts and provided mediation. I interfaced with other units on Post, as well as with our higher command. It was a busy year, and my learning curve went straight up.

During this time, I received a call from my personnel manager saying they needed someone to take command of one of the Joint Reserve Intelligence Centers (JRIC). He reviewed my records and said I would be a perfect fit. I considered it overnight and called him the next day and refused the offer. I told him I had only been in the Deputy position a couple months, and I was learning so much from the Commandant and I was not ready to leave yet. A couple months later, I received a notice announcing the Command Board was convening. This is a board meeting to select prospective officers for command— Captain (O-3) and Lieutenant Colonel (O-5) commands. I tossed the letter; I already told them I was not interested at this time.

During this period, I connected to my family. My older kids were getting on with their lives. Kelly and Amy were both married and starting families. I was lucky enough to be able to visit Kelly and her husband in San Diego after the birth of my first grandson. I was also able to take leave and help Amy out for a couple weeks after she had my first granddaughter. Kelly had moved to Iowa while I was stationed at the ARRTC. She had a home birth for her second child and when I got the call at work she was in labor, I dropped everything, took the boys, and arrived in time to witness the miracle of birth. I never believed I would have the opportunity to witness the birth of a baby after my own deliveries. I will always treasure this event; it was as emotional as seeing my own children come into the world. The birth of a child is a miracle.

The next summer, I took a vacation and went east with Joe and Frank for Bobby's wedding. Bobby had been dating Eva for a few years. So, I knew her and her family and was thrilled for the couple. They had hoped to get married after he finished Basic Training, but after training, Bobby was assigned to Korea. So, they put the wedding off for a year, until he returned. He returned to the States shortly before the wedding and would be assigned to Ft. Bragg. Although I was again on active duty and living away from Buffalo, I was close enough to be involved in the wedding. Plus, my role in my son's wedding was not as consuming as my role in my daughters' weddings. Additionally, both Joe and Frank were included in the wedding party. Bobby had bonded with the boys at SHAPE. He always maintained contact with them and wanted his two younger brothers to be in his wedding. They were important in his life, and they are still important to each other now. Bobby's father, Bob, and I had finally put our differences behind us and could get along amicably. It was a good thing, because at the rehearsal the priest kept referring to us as husband and wife, while we both corrected him with "Ex."

While in Buffalo for the wedding, I spent a lot of time with

Jacqie who, despite trying new treatments, was losing her fight with cancer. She was doing so poorly I was afraid I would be attending a funeral as well. This was back in the 1990s when breast cancer was the kiss of death to most women who were diagnosed. In the previous five years, I had lost four friends to breast cancer. However, Jacqie had tried experimental drugs and had fought the good fight, living years beyond her initial diagnosis. However, she was currently in hospice, on steroids as well as morphine. Miraculously, for a couple days in the middle of her pain and illness, she had a brief period of relief. She not only attended, but also danced, at my son's wedding. She was my best friend for years. We shared holidays when possible and she visited most places where I was stationed. We continued to talk on a weekly basis. A couple of weeks after the wedding, she called. She had just taken her pain meds, and she asked if we could talk until they kicked in? We had the best conversation, ending by telling each other how much we loved each other. The next day I received the phone call notifying me she had died. Having time with her during my Buffalo visit, seeing her smiling and dancing at Bobby's wedding, and talking the night before she died eased the grief and tremendous loss in losing this friend, confidant, and supporter of so many years. This loss left a huge impact on me. It took years before I allowed myself to get so close to another friend. Jacqie was the sister I never had. She was a beautiful human being.

I went to Buffalo for the funeral and upon returning home in the late afternoon, I decided to go into the office and check my emails before I officially returned to work the next day. There were notes all over my desk to call COL Robinett, and I was about to call him when he walked into my office. He sat and proceeded to tell me three members of our unit were selected for command: two of our captains got selected for Company Commands, and ME for a Battalion Command. I was shocked. Seems there was a letter of declination I had to sign if I did not want to be considered. It was in the letter regarding the command board I elected to toss. So, after two years in the AGR program, in August 1998, I was selected for a command.

I was chosen to command the Joint Reserve Intelligence Center (JRIC) at Ft. Sheridan, IL, north of Chicago. Shortly after my selection, I got a call from the outgoing Commander. During our conversation, he tried to convince me I was not ready for this job, and I was not prepared to handle this command. This provoked some uneasiness about what I was getting myself into.

Around the same time, I came out on the list announcing promotions to Lieutenant Colonel. As is the custom in the military, when you are promoted, YOU throw the party. Since you are making the big bucks, you can share it with your unit, family, and friends. As it turned out, my promotion coincided with my departure from the ARRTC. My parents came in for my promotion and party, but COL Robinett, who was going to promote me, got called out on a family emergency. So, I requested the Post Commander to do the honors, and he agreed. My father was there, and I wanted him to assist pinning on my Silver Oak leaf. I still remember his hand shaking as he pinned it on. We all went back to my house for my party. Even though I had only been at the ARRTC for two years, I had volunteered at the church, was an active parent with my kids, their friends, and families, and I was close with my neighbors and co-workers. Of course, I invited them all to my party. At one point on the day of the party, I looked, and cars were parked on both sides of the street, as far as I could see in both directions. I could not believe the response I had received to my invitation. The ARRTC had a farewell for me, and they roasted me. It was great and so much fun. It was July 1998, and I was again changing one assignment for another, this time as a Commander. I was on an upward trajectory at work. But I was also apprehensive. A command could make or break me. But I put those fears aside, and the boys and I went faithfully forward. Again.

14

Command: It's Good to be Queen

The Ft. Sheridan JRIC was indeed a hotbed of activity and issues. It was the highest profiled unit in the Army Reserves and was recognized within the Department of Defense as the premier, multi-service operational training and joint military intelligence production facility, supporting the National Agencies as well as the Warfighters. We filled significant gaps in military intelligence production at the highest levels of command. We were also involved in real world live missions in direct support to both Kosovo and Bosnia. This was the unit I was commanding.

Despite my trepidation, I jumped into command. I recognized not everyone gets a chance at command; this was an honor bestowed on me by leaders in the Army. Members of a command board are given stacks of military records to review. Every member of the board has their own qualifiers and discriminators for the first cut. It could be how the soldier looks in his/her military uniform (based on a picture in our file), or what kind of positions he/she has held, as well as what kind of ratings they have received. Many files are set aside with only a cursory glance. The remaining files are more carefully considered, and all the members of the board add scores to determine the top of the list. These people are offered a command. It is a privilege as well as a responsibility. I was more aware of the responsibility than the privilege. I had seen early in my career what could happen to officers who didn't measure up in their senior officers' eyes.

I had been on Active Duty for 9 years prior to coming back on active duty in the Active Guard and Reserve (AGR) program. I only had two years in the program when I was selected to command the Fort Sheridan Joint Reserve Intelligence Center (JRIC). Consequently, most AGR personnel did not know me. I found out later everyone at the JRIC was asking, "Who is this no-name coming to Command us?" It was to my advantage I did not know this when I arrived. Instead, I set about dealing with a change of command. In addition to my own change of command, there was a Navy unit, one of the Tenants of the JRIC, who also was having a change of command. This unit was commanded by a Navy Captain (equivalent to an Army Colonel), so we decided to do a joint ceremony. This was the first time I was able to experience some of the customs of another service, and it was great being a participant. The "side boys" blew a whistle while we all marched in. My boss was there to pass the guidon (unit flag) from the outgoing Commander to me, to signify the passing of command responsibility. As is the custom in the Navy, once the outgoing commander says his final farewell speech, he is "relieved of command" (which in the Army is a truly negative thing. But in the Navy, it is how relinquishing command is defined). Once relieved, he exits the room and is no longer a part of the festivities. Gone. Done. When I did my change of command at the end of my tour, I could see why this would be an advantage. All the people you interchange with are now more concerned about connecting and forming a relationship with the new commander; their connection to the old is no longer an asset. Time to move on.

The first order of business for me was to talk individually to key personnel. "Describe what you do within the organization, what are your main issues, and, from your perspective, what could be improved upon?" After talking to the personnel, the outgoing commander, and my boss, I was able to see my role and challenges more clearly. I was also able to determine who to go to for results. The difficult part would be taking the unit to the next level and getting it to perform optimally.

There were tenant units, from various commands and services, who were all vying for space and time within the Center. Many did not get along. It all fell on my shoulders to sort it out and resolve issues. The Navy originally conceived this Joint Reserve Intelligence Program concept. All the services were involved and operated their own centers, each supporting various service and joint organizations. The Navy was a full-time presence at the JRIC I commanded, and the biggest problems came from conflicting theories on how it should be run. The Navy believed in a more centralized control system. They looked to the Program Directors at Defense Intelligence Agency for guidance and direction. The Army (and my boss) believed control should be more decentralized and left to the individual services. I resolved this issue by gathering information, talking to the people involved and making the best decisions I could. Sometimes this meant defending myself to my boss and other times it meant defending myself to the Directors of the program. Maybe I could have commanded with a stronger hand, but this was not my style. And this was a joint operation. There was more to be gained by getting along, working together, and supporting one another than by fighting for service objectives. So, I started a monthly luncheon. One division or unit would provide food (hot dogs/hamburgers, spaghetti, tacos) and charge a small fee to cover the cost of food. We would order a cake for dessert, and we would celebrate all the birthdays in the month. It was a social event, and people took advantage of not leaving for lunch or bringing a sandwich from home. It took a while, but people with differing opinions sat with each other and talked. Ever so slightly, there seemed to be a growing sense of cohesion. This helped the different units come together into a highly effective team. We were recognized for our tactical and technical competence and our ability to provide high quality service, specifically tactical military intelligence training and production. This brought our center credibility and acclaim.

There were many mornings I would wake up and go to the 6:30 Mass and pray before work, "Dear God, help me, because I don't know what to do." This always brought me a sense of peace and helped me gain perspective on the issues. I had to make some difficult decisions, but they were working, and our center was prospering.

I also found that command had its perks. When I first came into the unit, if I happened to mention I would like a chair in my office, the next day it was there. Being in command was kind of like thinking something out loud, and it happens. What a nice surprise and benefit.

One tenant unit at the JRIC stands out in my memory. It was composed of members of the deactivated 12th Special Forces (SF) Group, now working together in a MID (Military Intelligence Detachment) and was commanded by COL Ted Drier. COL Drier was a tough, crusty SF type of soldier I loved working with. Not because he was easy to work with. He was one of those people who could make you feel dumber than a rock, by giving you this look. But over the years, he became one of the best mentors I ever had. Often when this MID had their weekend drills, I would be invited to join them for Saturday night dinner after drill, at the local Chinese restaurant. During these meals, I got to hear a lot of SF stories, as they drank and laughed about some of their escapades. They lived the expression, "It is easier to get forgiveness than permission," meaning they often did what was needed to get the mission accomplished, even if they didn't follow directives exactly. Their commanders knew this, and they usually received forgiveness.

It was during this time my son, Bobby, who was in the Army, went to the Special Forces (SF) Qualification Course—

the "Q" Course. This is a grueling course, physically and mentally demanding, separating the good from the best. Those who succeed continue to Special Forces Training. COL Drier would stop by and regularly ask if I had heard from my son. When I shook my head "no" he said, "Okay. Good. This is a good sign." Every day he would come by and ask. I would tell him "No" and every day he told me, "No news is good news." Finally, I got the call from my son; he had been selected. He was one of the best. He was one of 75 selected out of an original 250. When I saw my SF friend and told him the good news, he was as happy as I was. All the SF guys came by and celebrated, high-fiving me as if I had been selected. This was great. Bobby did all the work, and I was being congratulated. When Bobby finished the course, I hung on every word as he shared his experience with me. I was so proud of him. He told me about a particularly tough march, carrying their heavy load of equipment. A guy came to him and shared, "Rogers, every time I'm frustrated with all the equipment I have to carry and am fatigued under the weight, I look over and say to myself, 'Look, there's Rogers—he's half my size, and he's carrying the same load as I am.' This alone gave me the incentive to keep going." But, Bobby, forever the optimist, looked over at this big guy, "Thank God I don't have to carry all the extra body weight around as well as the equipment."

After most of the class had dropped out or failed, they had one more last long march. At the end, the remaining group was called to attention. They called names and divided the group. "Which group am I in? All of us survived the training. We all made it. Why are we being separated?" After going through all the training, living through the sleep and food deprivation, surviving the tremendous demands on your body and mind, this last separation eliminated all those who failed their peer evaluation. Can you imagine going through those weeks of hell, going when your body no longer listens to your mind, digging deep, only to fail because of the evaluation of your peers? I love this mentality, though. SF operates as a team, and if you can't depend on the guy next to you or your team members to do their part, it could negatively impact the whole mission. And now my son was going to be a Special Forces soldier, a Green Beret. He was the real soldier in the family. I paled in comparison.

When the SF MID Commander, COL Drier retired, all those who knew and loved him spent two hours straight roasting him at his retirement dinner. I was the only female who roasted him. My final comment was "Finally, after trying and failing to rise in the eyes of this tough and hard SF colonel, after doing all I could to impress him with my ability, I finally found the one thing I could do to elevate myself in his eyes. The one thing which put me on a par with these SF soldiers and made me an equal in this elite group. I found I had one capability gaining me the respect and admiration of these amazing men. The one thing I could do. . . I could give birth to and raise an SF soldier!" Everyone cheered. COL Drier was a great leader. Although I never worked for him, I worked with him in many of my positions, and I was honored to call him friend. He was the only and best mentor I had in the military. Unfortunately, during the writing of this book, this colonel passed away. He embodied all I loved about the Army. He should have died surrounded by all his SF friends, telling stories about earlier times, and toasting him, instead of in some hospital room. Thank you, Colonel Ted Drier for your life and service.

Traditionally, the wife of the Commander forms a Wives Group, so the wives could bond with the spouses of the men their husbands were working with. What do I do as a single female commander? I formed a Wives Group as well. I told the women, "I have to work and talk to your husbands all day long. I need some female companionship and conversation."

So periodically, I was able to step out of the role of Commander and host a group of women talking and doing "girl stuff." This was so much fun, and I made some outstanding friendships within this group.

For the most part, the people at work were great. Joe and Frank were attending a private school in Illinois. Students needed to provide their own transportation to and from school. So, I dropped them off on my way to work in the morning and, every afternoon, I would leave work to go get them, hear about their day, drop them at home, and return to work. Thank goodness, I lived on post, and the school was not far away. My staff knew not to plan meetings for this time of day, and there were even a couple times I might be in the middle of something, and I would get a gentle reminder, "Ma'am, It's three o'clock. Your kids are out of school. . ."

The boys met some great friends and had rewarding experiences during this time as well, particularly Joe who was caddying at a local country club. He did so well his first summer, he was not only named "Rookie of the Year" but also "Caddie of the Year" because he had completed more loops than any of the other caddies. The golf pro called me and told me the club selects a caddie every year and awards him an "Evans Scholarship." This is a scholarship established by Chic Evans, who was himself a caddie. The pro told me although Joe was not a "shoo-in," he was well liked by the members, and he had a good chance at earning the scholarship. However, Joe was only a freshman, and I told the pro, "I cannot stay here for my son's caddie career." However, the club offered to allow him to return every year and caddie for the summer after we moved on to my next assignment. Joe did, in fact, return every summer and ultimately won an Evans caddie scholarship to Northwestern University, which became a catalyst on his path to a successful life.

After being in command for two years, I came out on the list for the AWC (Army War College), starting in the summer of 2000. The AWC is a yearlong military school, located at Carlisle Barracks outside of Harrisburg, PA. We would be moving again.

Days before leaving, our dog, Sandy, was missing. My son, Frank, was devastated. He already was adept and had an inherent sense of how to use a computer. He researched online and, in his misery, won the sympathy of a Pet Detective Agency who offered to help him. Although they sent posters to all the local vets and dog grooming businesses, and Frank posted signs all over, we never found her. I did find out at some point, a member of my command was out running, and Sandy followed him back to the unit. After seeing one of the posters, he told me, "OMG! She's the same dog who followed me back from my run. I contemplated keeping her, but my wife would have killed me if I brought another dog home." He was the last one to see Sandy, and Frank had a particularly difficult time leaving without her. He was worried she might find her way home, and we would be gone.

My change of command was bittersweet. Looking back at my accomplishments, the enormity of what we had done as a unit, was staggering. I was so grateful and proud of the members of my command who had worked so hard and accomplished so much. We had formed an effective team, and we were a powerful force. Now I was turning the unit over to a new commander, who would take them even further. And I was moving on to the Army War College and another great opportunity, developing me and forming me for my assignments yet to come.

The highlight of my command was a social event. It was an official event with a social aspect. The Fort Sheridan JRIC was doing exceedingly well. We had one man who had an amazing talent in deciphering codes and who was often in the spotlight. This brought us to the attention of the Assistant Secretary of Defense (Intelligence) and other national intelligence agencies. As a result, during my command, funds were allocated for us to expand and build a new wing, with new equipment, new bandwidth, new communications, and new capabilities. This was a yearlong endeavor and was finally completed, shortly before my departure. We hosted a ribbon cutting ceremony, not only to showcase our new addition, but also to highlight our new and expanding capabilities. We decided to go all out and make it an event worthy of our hard work and accomplishments over the past few years, as well as for the high-level visitors who would be attending. However, it was the end of the fiscal year and funding for ceremonies was non-existent. We knew generals and Senior Executive Service (SES-high level civilians) were coming from all over the world (from units we supported at our site), including the Assistant Secretary of Defense. So, I went to the wives' group and requested their help. Not surprising, the wives' group came through. Together we put together an event far exceeding anything an expensive caterer could have prepared. Not only did they provide an amazing spread for our guests, consisting of delicious homemade dishes, but they also came and helped set a beautiful presentation on linen covered tables, adorned with centerpieces, and they themselves served. They turned out to be the best addition to a remarkable event. As a bonus, these terrific women got a seldom-seen peek into their spouse's world.

The ribbon cutting ceremony was a huge success. The high-level officers we invited were impressed with the facility and even more so with the work we were accomplishing there. Ft. Sheridan became the poster child for the other JRICs already in place and those about to be opened. After my introductory briefing, one of the generals gave me a coin. My son Bobby had recently told me about his coins, and I mentioned to the general my son had a bunch of coins, and this one was the first I had ever received. All the generals started to pull coins out of their pockets, and I walked away with about 10 coins. Coins are designed by the Commander and Sergeant

Major of a unit and are given out as an "Atta boy" or a "Thank you." As is the custom, if you are out drinking with someone who gave you a coin, and he lays his coin on the table, if you don't have yours, drinks are on you. It's a great custom and is still being practiced, despite the fact it became an "unauthorized expense" for Commanders, and now they must pay out of pocket if they desire to award coins.

This ribbon cutting ceremony, inclusive of the amazing spread we were able to provide for our distinguished guests, brought recognition and credit to the incredible people who worked at the Fort Sheridan JRIC. The impact of the details and components of the ceremony along with the attention and recognition of our distinguished guests cannot be understated. For me personally, the names of people added to my address book served me especially well later when I spent the last four years of my career working in Washington, DC, where I interfaced with many of these people on a regular basis. This was a great achievement in my two-year command. Now it was time to move on to the Army War College.

15

Introspection: A Two-Edged Sword

This was not any army school–this was the Army War College, training those who a board determines have the potential for General Officer or Senior Executive Service. I was told it is more difficult to be selected for the Army War College (AWC) than it is to be selected for promotion to Colonel. So, when I first found out I was selected, I was gloating to myself, "I'm cool, I'm the man" kind of attitude. However, when I got there and looked around the class, I was humbled by the experiences and assignments some of my classmates had. My own modest career paled in comparison. For sure some dreadful error had been made, and I had been sent by mistake. If I wasn't careful, I would blow my cover and be sent home.

There was one guy in my seminar (section) who, as an enlisted soldier, was selected for Special Forces (SF). After completing his commitment, he left the Army and went to college and medical school. He came back on Active Duty, as an officer and medical doctor in SF. He must have seen a lot of action because his uniform could hardly hold all his medals. He was impressive, but everyone was. I was in awe of the people in my seminar—so much talent, so much knowledge. These people were being groomed for general officer positions.

I was looking forward to a year of schooling and time for introspection. My career was moving along, my finances were stable, and my family seemed to be doing well. It was an honor and a blessing to spend a year in this school receiving advanced professional education for senior military officers and their counterparts in other federal agencies and foreign armies. The program culminated in a master's degree in strategic studies. The instruction focused on war fighting strategy and national security policy. We learned through lectures, seminar presentations and discussions, and individual research. We examined the nature of leadership to include ethics; we studied US national security policy, national military strategy and the strategic decision-making process. We culminated with an exercise at the end of the year, where we applied everything we learned to a simulated world crisis.

There were so many great aspects to the training we received at the AWC. I loved the way the seminars (small groups of about 20 members who stayed together for the duration of the AWC year) were compiled. Each seminar consisted of representatives from the combat arms, combat support, and service support, the Reserves/National Guard, female military members, Air Force, Navy/Marines, Department of Defense Civilians, and Foreign Military Officers. Within the seminar, we had a tremendous amount of reading, which we later discussed in class. The mix of people in the seminar from such diverse areas of interest resulted in extremely lively and informative discussions. In my seminar, I had an Air Force pilot seated on one side of me and a SF soldier on the other, both outstanding men and great warriors. The youngest member of my seminar was a Navy man who I developed a deep respect for, simply because he was so open to listening to other people and asking some especially provocative questions. He went on to become Admiral. Fifteen out of twenty-two members of our seminar became general officers.

Leadership was the focus of our studies, and we examined people who exhibited the aspects of a great leader. First and foremost, great leaders have a strategic vision, which inspires and motivates their subordinates. Second, leaders know how to instill in their subordinates a belief their contribution was important and necessary. Third, they know how to create teams and use each person's strengths. Fourth, they train their successors, to ensure permanence and continuity, so accomplishments and achievements do not end when they leave. We were assigned to write and report on a strategic leader, demonstrating these qualities. Many were choosing obvious leaders: Lincoln, MacArthur, and Martin Luther King Jr. There were plenty of great leaders to choose from. I was inspired to write my paper on Mother Theresa. Mother Theresa, with no personal funding, built hospitals and homes where the sick and homeless of India could be fed, housed, and medically treated. She was not about converting them, but about treating each person with dignity, respect, and love. She had a vision and was unstoppable in accomplishing it. The people who worked for and with her did so with love. When important or famous people requested some time with her or reporters requested an interview, they had to help serve her clientele for a time before she would make time for them. As her pursuit grew, she needed people to manage resources, keep track of her clients and their needs, do fund raising, and all other aspects of running a business. She built teams of people to do this. And finally, she chose and trained her successor. She was successful, influential, and she made an impact. She embodied all the qualities of a great leader. She can be counted among the great strategic leaders of our time.

One of the biggest benefits of this year of academia was it allowed all of us to seriously consider what our strengths and weaknesses were, and what kind of leaders we wanted to be. I developed my own personal philosophy of leadership. I knew as a leader, I had to accept responsibility for not only the noteworthy things the people under me accomplished, but I also had to accept responsibility for their failures. I learned I could make tough decisions if I had to, and I could hold people accountable. I had an obligation to take care of the people under my leadership, to provide them what they needed to accomplish their job in the organization. Finally, I wanted the people I led to know they could trust me, that I was reliable and a person of integrity.

As I was using this year to determine what kind of officer I would be going forward, Joe and Frank were shaping their own futures. I raised them to be independent, both by my example and also what I expected of them. Joe was always focused and driven. As a baby, he always stood out with his red hair and freckles. Even with older kids, it seemed he would always take control and become the leader. I saw this in him as young as eight years old. He adored his older brother Bobby and, with his encouragement, tried practically every sport and excelled at most. From a young age, he was industrious. His first business venture was in 6th grade, making and selling holiday wreaths. He was astute and intently tuned in to the world around him. He soaked in all the information he could glean from the people he caddied for at Old Elm.

Frank could have used more guidance and direction from me. I never gave this to any of my children. I always told them they were smart and if they worked hard, they would be rewarded with good grades and opportunities. I believed poorer grades were a result of not putting enough effort forth. This did not work well for Frank. He was more sensitive than Joe, not as driven, but every bit as capable—when he applied himself. if the drive came from within, it would be much more valuable than if I demanded results. He was a little older before he applied himself and reaped the benefits. Now as an adult, he has done amazingly well financially and professionally, while caring about people and helping subordinates climb the corporate ladder with him.

My next assignment after the Army War College was in Washington, DC. Joe immediately checked out the schools in the area, before I even decided which area we were going to live in. He discovered the countrywide high ratings of Thomas

Jefferson School of Science and Technology in Alexandria, VA, and this was where he set his sights. They only admitted four new students as sophomores, decided by SAT scores taken as a freshman. Joe was one of the four sophomores admitted. He was setting his trajectory going forward and establishing goals, driven by something within, not asking any help, only support from me. I was fooling myself. Joe didn't ask for help because he knew I wouldn't have the information he was looking for. I still had the narrow ideas about education I was raised with. Joe had insights I lacked, and he had to do it for himself.

At the War College, we frequently had presentations and briefings by various general officers, SESs, and political figures collectively in our auditorium, aptly labeled "the big red bedroom," not only because of the red upholstered seats and red carpeting, but because no matter what time of the day it was, there was something about the room causing many of us to immediately fall asleep. I was no exception; I would take caffeine, I would bring gum to chew, I would focus on taking notes, but inevitably, the eyelids would get heavy, and I would catch myself jerking awake before I had nodded off. One morning we had a four-star general briefing us. It was the day after the election in 2000; a friend had stayed up till the bitter end tracking it. She was seated about three rows from the front of the room this particular morning. She was a smart woman who was always engaged in the briefings, but this morning her body resisted any effort to stay awake. Suddenly the General belts out, "Will someone wake the Air Force Lieutenant Colonel?" The rest of us all sat straight in our seats, because, of course, it could have been any one of us. She later confided the only thing worse would have been if he yelled, "Will someone wake the FEMALE Air Force Lieutenant Colonel!" The poor thing. No one let her forget it, even years later, making jokes about her chair winning a huge amount of money at an AWC auction. At the end of the year, we all gathered in The Big Red Bedroom and a video came on the screen.

It was a collection of clips from the monitors in the room over the course of our year, focusing on individuals who fell asleep during presentations in the room. The clips went on and on, concluding with clips of some of our instructors asleep.

We had a certain number of electives we could take. There were two electives I loved. The first was a Toastmasters course. The second was a course entitled "The Human Dimension of Men in Battle" taught by a Special Forces officer. The latter was by far my favorite course at the War College. We met twice a week and at every class we were responsible for giving a report on an assigned book we had read. We each read a different book, so we could not depend on someone else to carry us.

The books were divided into topics: the Revolutionary War, the Civil War, World Wars I and II, the Vietnam War, and the Korean War. We looked at war from the journalist's/correspondent's point of view, as well as from the Air Force and Navy perspectives. I am not a history buff, but I LOVED this course. The books I read were phenomenal. I would get carried away giving my book report, encouraging my classmates to run out and read the book themselves. At the end of the course, we had to write a paper on why these authors would write about the human dimension of men in battle rather than simply the battle tactics and strategies examined in after action reports. I believe there were several reasons. The first is the therapeutic value of looking at the experience. Post-Traumatic Stress Disorder (PTSD) has been around for years, referred to by many different names. Looking back on these experiences and analyzing them to the extent needed to write an account helped some military warriors to gain a perspective on the experience allowing them to function and live with the trauma. This includes recognizing their lives will never again be the same and they will be impacted by the experience of battle for the rest of their lives. Another reason a warrior may write about a battle or experience is to "set the record straight." I believe this is especially true of wars such as the Vietnam War for Americans or World War II for the Germans, when the political basis was controversial and the criticism rampant. These writers tried to justify their desire to fulfill their patriotic duty, ideals they were taught as a child, ideals which were the essence of the nation's reason for existence, only to find their own leaders had misled them. Their books are a plea to the world not to discount their service, their mutilations, their horrors, and their deaths because the political motivations of the country were not pure. The final reason for writing these books is to examine another dimension of the human psyche. These writers desire to explain the "Why?" There are books about the tactics of war, the strategy of war, but it is in reading books about the human dimension of war and battle that we grasp the "Why." Why would a man die for his country or for his buddy in the foxhole? Why would he go on missions day after day where he continually puts himself in harm's way. Why does he stay with his unit, when it is unbearably cold or hot, when he is infested with lice, when the stench of injuries and death is a daily companion. What urges him on when the meals, if they come, often result in dysentery, when all his senses experience the contamination of the battlefield around him. Why a man, when leaving a unit he faced battle with, is filled with an overpowering sadness when he finally comes home and is numb to the joy of seeing his wife and new baby. This leaves him with irreconcilable emotions. I became immersed when I read these stories, and I found the resulting discussions were deeply emotional and extremely provocative. As I now look back on my career, the human dimension of men in battle has often colored my perspectives.

At the end of the year, we had an exercise to test what we learned at school. Each of us played roles as military leaders (in our specialty) or government officials, all the way to the POTUS (President of the United States) and Vice President, including Secretary of State, Secretary of Defense, Congressman, Chiefs of Staffs of the Army, Navy and Air Force, news broadcasters and journalists, Department of Health, and representatives of various other "mover and shaker" groups. I was assigned the position of Assistant Secretary of Defense for Intelligence. During this exercise, every evil imaginable confronts the US. We were on the verge of war with China. North Korea was challenging us again. The Middle East was a hotbed of terrorists. There was genocide in Africa, famine in India, a hurricane had recently devastated Puerto Rico. We had to make decisions on how to deal with each of these crises. We had our own Public Affairs Officers who interviewed various officials throughout the day. We had news broadcasts on our closed-circuit TVs daily throughout the exercise. The media blips included commentaries on decisions we were making to deal with the crises at hand but also contained some humorous clips and side notes. During the exercise, many of the real people who we were representing came by to check in and give their perspective on what they would do. It was a fascinating exercise. What a great way to end the year and to conclude the course with a master's in Strategic Studies was the icing on the cake. As was the case with so many of the important events in my life, my parents, as well as other family and friends, came to my graduation, sharing again in my success.

Ironically, during this time of learning and development, my introspection resulted in a period of self-doubt. For the first time in my career, I questioned whether I even belonged in the Army. Was I truly cut out to be the kind of leader higher ranks would demand? Would I have the wisdom, intelligence, and tenacity to make the decisions a general must make? In addition, I was isolated, even though I was the social chair for my seminar, and I planned family parties and acknowledged birthdays within the seminar. Maybe it was because I lived off-post, maybe because I was female, or maybe it was some mid-life thing I was going through. However, when I shared this with other classmates, I found I was not alone. There were several of my classmates who were experiencing similar emotions. In fact, some were on medication for their depression.

It was surprising to me in this great academic environment of mental stimulation, we would find any reason to be discouraged.

As I was struggling with my own life, my youngest son Frank, was quietly, despairingly going through his own introspection. He confided to me many years later this was also an especially difficult time for him. Since I had come back on active duty four years prior in 1996, this was the third time the Army moved us. Frank was more sensitive, and it was difficult for him to leave the familiar and start over someplace new. I knew he was still grieving the loss of our dog, but I was not aware of how much this impacted him. He reasoned since I had so much on my plate, he wouldn't bother me with his problems. Frank did not have the resiliency Joe had, and the moves were taking a toll on him. He needed more stability and hated having to say goodbye to friends. He was not involved in sports, so he often found it difficult to find his niche in a new school, with a new group of people. I now see I was so immersed in my own experience at the time, I did not notice my child's needs. I was not living to my own standard as a mom. I can't help asking if every career mother goes through this. Or is this a single parent phenomenon? Or was it me?

And, if this wasn't enough, during this period, sometime prior to graduation, my daughter Kelly and her husband, Mike, cut all ties with both of their immediate, as well as extended families, which included parents, siblings, grandparents, aunts, uncles, and cousins. Again, Kelly left a large hole in our lives, especially for her brothers and sister; they were always so close. Although everyone had conjectures why she would do this, we unfortunately had no explanation. We were all left with a huge void.

This was an excellent professional opportunity for me. I earned a master's degree, had an opportunity to analyze and explore my leadership techniques and was mentally challenged in my classes. At the time my family was doing well. The girls were married and starting their own families and I was able to enjoy my grandchildren. At the time, I had no idea Kelly's estrangement from the family would continue for many years. I did not know about Frank's struggles until much later. Joe was doing well in school and was following his own trajectory. Looking back, was it my inability to balance my career and my family or was it the demands the military places on us, which filter to our families, in sometimes especially subtle, but also in terribly alarming ways? Was the profession I chose because it fostered family cohesion, in reality hurting it? I take responsibility for my family, but I cannot help questioning the impact of military requirements as well.

16

Washington, DC: Work and Family Experiences

9/11 happened shortly after I arrived at my next assignment in Washington, DC. The Defense Intelligence Agency (DIA) offices where I worked were in Clarendon, VA. However, my boss came directly under the Assistant Chief of Staff (Intelligence) who was located at the Pentagon, so my time was divided between the two locations. On the day of the attack, I was at the Clarendon office. We had a TV there with the news running continuously. Somebody noticed the newscast of the first plane hitting the twin towers in NYC and called us in. Instantaneously, we saw the second plane hit, which confirmed this was not an accident. I remember how surreal it all seemed. Maybe this was a modern day H.G. Wells, the "War of the Worlds." Minutes later came the news that the Pentagon was hit, and as we moved to our window on the 11th floor, we could see the smoke rising into the sky from the Pentagon. Almost immediately, we were told to evacuate the building. We had no idea at the time if the attacks would continue to other DC office buildings, and/or across the country. Since the Metro had immediately ceased running, and roads were blocked all over, we went to the home of a co-worker, who lived blocks away. There we continued to watch the news on TV. The phone lines were all busy, but I was finally able to get a message out to my kids confirming I was okay. It was only later I found out they were glued to the TVs at school, worrying, "Was this one of the days my mom was at the Pentagon?" It took me until 10 p.m. to finally get home; it was a nerve-wracking day for all of us.

The remains of the bodies from the Pentagon attack were all shipped to Dover Air Force Base (AFB), Delaware and it was there forensics went to work, accumulating body parts and personal effects, identifying the bodies, and notifying the services, who notified the next of kin. Once funeral arrangements were made, each casket had an escort of equal or higher rank, to bring the casket home. I was one of these escorts. When body parts were all assembled, they were wrapped in a military blanket, and the military member's Class A uniform (dress uniform) was placed on top, with all his medals. When I was given the personal effects of the Lieutenant Colonel I was escorting home to deliver to his family at the funeral home, I noted his watch was still ticking and keeping time. This seemed like such a bizarre contrast to the mutilated body wrapped in the blanket and laid in the casket. Every effort was made to pay fitting tribute to these service members: as the casket was loaded into the hearse, everyone around stopped what they were doing, came to attention, and saluted. As the hearse weaved through the streets on the Dover AFB installation, people all stopped, came to attention, and saluted. They had no way of knowing if therein lay an officer or enlisted. It didn't matter. They died in service to their country, and they deserved the utmost respect. I accompanied the casket to the funeral home in southern Virginia, where it was passed to the waiting family. I met the family and passed on the personal effects of their loved one. I quietly and soberly made my way back to DC, deeply moved and touched by this experience and not sure what to do with my sorrowful emotions.

My job at DIA was Operations Officer in DIA's Reserve Intelligence Integration Division (RIID). I wore three hats in this assignment. My first hat was as the Army liaison officer (LNO) to DIA, providing advice and expertise to the DIA staff regarding the utilization and integration of Army intelligence resources for meeting DoD intelligence requirements. My second hat was as the Operations Officer for the unit, managing and overseeing the Navy, Air Force, Marine and National Guard liaison officers. My third hat was as the DIA liaison to Army and Joint Commands. As a liaison officer, I had to coordinate across as well as up and down the Intelligence spectrum; however, I also had to complete a lot of writing. I wrote a handbook for operations officers at the JRIC sites. I was also deeply involved in the writing of the regulation governing the Under Secretary of Defense for Intelligence (USDI) which was a new office being established to put all the intelligence agencies (the Service intelligence agencies, as well as the CIA) under one umbrella.

My job brought me a lot of visibility within the Intelligence Community in DC. As a result, I was approached by members of the Army Reserve Intelligence Community to address the interests of Military Intelligence to the Chief of Army Reserves (CAR). The CAR was considering combining the Intelligence (G-2) section with the Operations (G-3) section. When a decision from the CAR seemed imminent, I approached my boss, and she encouraged me to put together a briefing, highlighting the contributions of Reserve Component Intelligence to the Warfighters, which I did. She made an appointment with the CAR. She was a Senior Executive Service (SES) member at DIA at the time, so equal in rank to the CAR. I presented my briefing to the CAR, exchanged a few more pleasantries, and left. Thereafter, not only were the two sections not combined, but the G2 remained its own entity. In fact, within a year, a whole new intelligence organization, the Military Intelligence Reserve Command (MIRC), was established—a huge accomplishment for Reserve Military Intelligence. I'm not saying my briefing made the difference, but, yes, I will take at least partial credit. Whatever I briefed to the General, it worked.

While I was enjoying my military position, the boys were

moving forward, both in high school. Joe had been tested and accepted into Thomas Jefferson School of Science and Technology—a magnet school for a select group of students from DC and Northern Virginia. It was obvious early on Joe would work hard and achieve great accomplishments in life. Frank was attending the local high school. We bought the largest house we ever had. It had four bedrooms, a living room, family room, dining room, and a finished basement. I had learned large homes aren't always great for family unity. If kids have their own rooms with their own televisions and their own computers, they could go days without interacting with their parents or each other. So, although the kids had their own rooms, the computer was in the family room adjacent to the kitchen. There were no laptops yet. As a mom, this worked much better—I could be preparing dinner, while one of the boys was on the computer, and we were all in the same proximity. We purchased only one TV, a big screen TV, and we put it in the recreation area in the basement. Living with one TV forced us to adjust and compromise, but, ultimately, it was a good move for all of us.

Kelly's withdrawal was sadly impacting our lives. The boys missed sharing their lives and activities with Kelly and her family, and I missed talking to them and staying in touch. Additionally, for her own reasons, Amy cut off communication, but only with me. This was a blow to me, and I did not know what to do. I remembered every mistake I made as a mom, but how could any of it justify estrangement? I put together a prayer corner. It was a quiet, inspirational space, with flowers, some written meditations, and some religious symbols to help me focus. I would pray there every morning before going to work. And I would cry. I cried a lot. By the time I got to work, I was all cried out. I was haunted with questions: why wouldn't they talk to me? I apologized for everything. Was there something I missed? Why were they keeping my grandchildren from me? Why? Why? Why? This loss was so overwhelming and the most difficult thing I could imagine. We were so close as a family. What happened? Thankfully, this assignment was much less demanding than command, and there were people at work I could talk to about my situation. I met regularly with a counselor. At first, she was hopeful, but as years went by, she became concerned about the impact this was having on me. She told me, "Carol, this is eating at you, and you have to let it go. Your daughters are in their own world and have their own issues. You have to find some peace with it." It didn't happen right away, but through the years I have tried to accept where they are, without attaching my own meaning to it.

I made a decision greatly impacting our family. The church requested families to take an exchange student for a year. For some reason, I was drawn to the information table and, on an impulse, I selected Mauricio, a young man from Bogota, Colombia, to come and live with the boys and me. All excited, I joined the boys in the car and announced my news. They both looked at me in horror asking, "Are you crazy? Why would you do this? We fight all the time, and you are at work. Why would you invite someone else into our home?" But this is exactly what I did, and it turned into an amazing experience for all of us. I would awake and go to work in the morning, and Joe would leave early to go to school. Mauricio and Frank attended the same high school and Mauricio's companionship was a bonus for Frank at his school. I would come home from work and we would all have dinner together. We integrated him in all aspects of our lives—he shared responsibilities with Joe and Frank and when I had leave from work, he would travel with us.

Joe and Frank were as different as night and day, and they did in fact fight with each other, but Mauricio became a buffer between them. Also, Joe was the oldest son at home, and saw himself as the "man" of the house, and in comes Mauricio, a year older than Joe. Mauricio immediately charmed me, making Joe resentful and maybe a little jealous, and Mauricio immediately bonded with Frank like a brother. However, by the time the holidays came, Joe relented to Mauricio's persistence, and the two became good friends. He, surprisingly, was a welcome addition to our home and family. We all grew closer together during this year and have remained friends and in contact with Mauricio ever since. I have no doubt I was guided to the table and this particular young man who impacted our lives and was part of our family for a year. Work was manageable for me, and it was a good time for us to have this exchange student.

Joe was playing football at high school. His brother, Bobby, came from North Carolina to Virginia for every one of his games during Joe's senior year. Bobby was devoted to his brothers and being a part of their lives. The school needed help from the parents for the football team home games, so I volunteered. However, the only position they had left was on the chain gang, holding the markers indicating the yardage of the play on the field during the football game. When I told Joe, he grunted, "Well, don't come in a dress and heels." (I may have put on a battle-dress uniform and boots for work, but I still enjoyed dressing as a girl.)

While Joe was playing football, Frank was in the basement developing his entrepreneurial and technical skills. He was taking apart broken computers, rebuilding them, and selling them on eBay. (I did not know about this until years later.) Frank's intellectual genius revealed itself in its own way and time. Like his mom, he had a relatively slow start, but soon passed his peers and rose to accomplish amazing things in his adult life. His grades were always good, but as a child he could never rationalize trading perfectly good playtime to study. He has carried his love of games and fun into his adult life. He is an extremely successful professional and now has the latest and greatest in fun things to do. He also married Stephanie, who shares his love of playtime with him, challenging him in video games and "one-wheeling." She is perfect for him. This is admirable in a world so focused on working hard, play is often forgotten.

Frank had a difficult time focusing as a child. As an adult he was diagnosed with mild attention deficit disorder. Maybe it manifested when he was younger, but neither his teachers nor I caught it. He had the biggest heart I have ever seen in a child. He still seems to see into people's souls and finds things to love others sometimes miss, regardless of how they look on the outside. His friends were always important to him, and I challenge anyone to compete with the vast number of his Facebook friends. He maintains those relationships to this day, often not only with friends and classmates, but with their siblings and parents as well.

Frank came to me at the end of his sophomore year of school with hopefulness and expectation. He found a place where he could get his high school diploma online and not go back to Hilton High School, which he hated, especially after Mauricio left. My first response was not only "No" but "Hell, no."

But he persisted and wanted to discuss it. I agreed and made a list of conditions which would end the discussion: it has to be an accredited program; the diploma must be recognized by prospective colleges; he must join some kind of social team (sports, art, music, etc.) to have the experience of working with others on a team; he needed to find a way to have interactions with different adults, so he could learn how to get along with authority. When we sat to talk, he already had the answers to all the issues I listed, and he concluded he would maintain a 3.5 average before I told him I would expect a 3.0. I finally agreed to let him try it. He succeeded, and this was how he finished high school. This worked for both of us in later assignments and deployments.

17

Life Experiences: Fate or Planned?

While I was at DIA, I came out on the list for promotion to O-6—Full Bird Colonel. I am still amazed as I look back at my career, the seemingly random moves bringing me to a point where I would be promoted to a Colonel in the US Army. Even though my first assignment back on Active Duty was in a low-visibility job as an instructor, my boss believed in me and gave me the flexibility to carve my own niche, resulting in me being selected for the Deputy Commandant position. This looked good when my records went before the command board, and I was selected for command. Having a good record and having a command postured me for selection for the AWC, which resulted in promotion to Colonel on June 11, 2003.

At this level, your assignment manager no longer makes the decision, but a board convenes to decide the assignments of the Colonels selected for promotion. I received orders to move into an O-6 billet at the Department of the Army, G-2 (Intelligence) which was located at the Pentagon. The G-2 three-star general was going to do the honors of promoting me. I was to meet him for the first time 30 minutes prior to the ceremony, so he could become familiar with me before the ceremony.

I was doing well in the military. I was considered successful. But I had this hidden life of a mother whose daughters were estranged from me. When I prepared for my promotion and my new unit inquired who would attend from my family, I simply answered, "My three sons," omitting the fact I had two daughters and five grandchildren who knew nothing about my life or me. I lived with the fear that if these people in my first assignment as a Colonel knew about this, it would tarnish my image as an effective officer.

As my promotions moved me to higher ranks, my parties grew as well, and this was no exception. I planned a big party at my house in Woodbridge, Virginia after my promotion ceremony, and I had a lot of family and guests coming in from out of town. I had taken care of everything, but I was late leaving the house, so I was stressed and harried. My nephew, Brian was following me when suddenly, he pulled over—his car was overheating. He had his wife and three kids, so there was no way they would fit in my car. I had to leave them. Sadly, they ultimately missed the ceremony. But I was already late for my meeting with the general. I finally got to the Pentagon, raced in, sweat pouring from my face, my uniform blouse streaked with streams of sweat, and went to see the general. He was great, calmed me, talked with me a little, straightened my uniform and walked me to the conference room. The general painted a nice picture of my background, especially considering the only things he knew about me were the questions I answered on the fly as we walked to the conference room. I know I spoke, but I have no idea what I said. Everyone formed a line to congratulate me and went back to the house for my party, and Monday it was back to work at my new job.

The board assigned me to Army G2. However, the G2 assigned me to the position of Chief, Operations Division, Intelligence Plans and Operations Directorate, Office of the Deputy Chief of Staff for Intelligence, Headquarters, Department of the Army in the Pentagon. I had to put all of this in—doesn't it sound impressive? Me, the skinny kid from Orchard Park, had the opportunity to work at the Pentagon. It was an incredible experience.

The Pentagon is huge. At the time, it housed some 27,000 uniformed and civilian personnel assigned to the Department of the Defense. If you were to walk around every ring and every corridor on all 5 floors, you would cover 27.1 miles. At one time or another, I covered every one of those miles, as there were people all over the Pentagon I had to find and interface with. The headquarters for each of the services were located there. They each had their own wing, commemorating their great leaders and their campaigns. There is a hall commemorating the military members who signed the Declaration of Independence. There is a section dedicated to DoD civilians. Since I arrived there after 9/11, there was a hall displaying some of the quilts schools, churches, and organizations made and sent. Additionally, there is the Pentagon Memorial Chapel, inside the Pentagon, and the 9/11 Memorial outside. Both are beautifully done and well worth a visit. The Pentagon itself is unbelievably rich in history. During the cold war, the Russians were convinced we had an underground operations center at the Pentagon. They had satellites watching us. They noticed people were walking to and from a central location in the courtyard inside the Pentagon at all hours of the day and night, so they decided this must be the entrance to the underground site. For years they had a missile aimed at this location. Truth is, it was a hot dog stand in the courtyard and was proudly referred to as "the deadliest hot dog stand in the world!"

My job carried with it a myriad of responsibilities, all designed to support the operational intelligence needs of the Army deployed to respond to crises around the world. One responsibility was to sit in on weekly meetings held by the G-3 (Operations). Officers from various offices were there, pleading their case for more money for fuel, or tactical vehicles, ammunition, people, training, and supplies. They were also delineating and making a case for their requirements for Operation Iraqi Freedom (OIF), which was currently underway. Some units deployed needing equipment, both individual and unit. This meeting was the place where all these requirements were discussed and prioritized and weighed against budget constraints. It was a real eye opener. I could not believe we were sending soldiers into a combat area and they did not have the funding for up-armored vehicles, which would protect the passengers from attack, especially since improvised explosive devices (IED) were becoming widely used in the Middle East.

General Cody, the Army G-3 (Operations), chaired this meeting. He was the kind of leader his soldiers would follow to hell and back and thank him for the opportunity to make the trip. The people who worked for him adored him. He was tough and demanding, but he was knowledgeable, fair, and could cut through the bullshit to get to the heart of any problem. He was focused on his responsibilities for Operational aspects of the Global War on Terrorism (GWOT) not only because he was dedicated to the Army, but also, he had a personal interest as he had two sons in the military who were both deployed to the Middle East at the time.

I had one disappointment about a year after arriving at the G-2. It was common knowledge the AWC groomed senior military and civilians for general officers or senior executive staff, respectively. However, when I became eligible to be considered for promotion to General, I received a letter stating my records would not be reviewed for the next General Officer promotion board because of date of birth (DOB). My birth year was before the cut-off. I was mortified, not necessarily because I expected to be selected, but because I was not being considered. I was being disqualified without my records being evaluated. I would rather be evaluated and told I'm not good enough than told I wasn't in the running because I was too old. I'll never know how I ranked with my peers.

My job did have some perks: one day the G-2 called me in. Princess Aisha of Jordan was coming to town, and she would like to learn about females in the US Army. She was an officer in the Jordanian Army. The General wanted me to schedule a presentation and a roundtable discussion for her, so I gathered some other female officers and a couple female Non-Commissioned Officers. The princess was amazing. Besides being beautiful, she was assured and confident. We exchanged stories of our training experiences and our assignments and the attitude of male soldiers towards us. It was fascinating to hear even though she was a princess, she did not get any special treatment at Basic Training. If anything, the instructors were harder on her because of her status. She had her Executive Officer with her, another female, and they joked about how they escaped the watchful eyes of their security detail so they could go shopping at Tysons Corner. The day concluded with dinner at the General's house. It was so easy to talk to her and she was so personable. I was moved by her warm invitation to come visit her in Jordan anytime. I was so sorry I was never able to act on her invitation.

During this time, Frank was working on his high school diploma online and was doing well. Joe had graduated from high school in 2004 and had applied and been accepted at Northwestern University. His Evans scholarship covered most of his tuition and expenses; additionally, housing, as the Evans House, on Fraternity Row was provided to these scholarship winners. On one of his trips home, he brought some friends from school and I was able to give them a tour of the Pentagon. My security badge allowed me to get into the Pentagon and to bring guests in. It was great to be able to share my workplace not only with my son, but with his friends as well. One of my responsibilities with the G2 was to oversee the Crisis Action Team in the Army Operations Center, which was manned 24/7. This was where information came in from around the world—televisions going constantly, news being pumped in from military installations around the world. This is where the Secretary of Defense and Chiefs of Staff were briefed on volatile situations. As part of the tour, I took them to the Army Operations Center. They got to sit in the chairs the generals sat in for critical briefings and were given a sample (unclassified) briefing. They were able to see a snapshot of the Pentagon few people have a chance to see.

I often had to go into the Pentagon on Saturdays or holidays. Sometimes I had a project deadline, or the General (G-2) would require a briefing. Often, I had to fill in for the General at the Saturday morning briefings with the military members deployed in support of the Global War on Terrorism. This meeting was headed by LTG Cody (the G-3) and included staff sections and reps from the units and Major Commands (MACOMS). We video-conference with the units in Iraq and Afghanistan. Discussions included highlights from the last week, after action reports from various operations, and a casualty count. The intelligence reports were of particular interest to the G-2 and me. It was a two-way exchange of information between deployed units and all of us supporting them back home.

After about a year working in this environment, I was compelled to volunteer to do my time in Iraq. Why now? A couple things happened: the horrible scandal at Abu Ghraib hit the news. Guards were using unauthorized methods of interrogating prisoners. I was troubled and disturbed by the whole thing. How could American soldiers ever get to the point they would participate in something so out of line with our values? In my opinion, all of us officers created an environment where this could happen. Every time we did not hold people to the standards, every time we looked the other way when soldiers were out of line and did not hold them accountable, every time we glossed through training, instead of emphasizing ethics and responsibility, we lowered the bar on what was expected from our soldiers. The Army, and specifically Military Intelligence, needed to heal from this incident, and maybe there was some way I could help foster this in Iraq. I recognized in this whole incident another aspect of the human dimension of men in battle. It resonated with me. Also, I was nearing the end of my career, and I had not been to Iraq or Afghanistan, and it was my turn. It would have been an unbelievable hardship if I had been deployed earlier in my career. Either the kids would have been uprooted from school and would have had to go back to Buffalo to stay with my parents, or my parents would have to leave their home and come to my home, according to my dependent care plan. Either way would have disrupted the lives of people I loved. But I was blessed I didn't have to. But now I can.

The first time I approached my kids, they were immediately upset. Frank was not looking forward to the upheaval in his life. Joe was afraid something might happen to me, and how would he deal with it? Drop out of school and join the Army himself to get retribution? This was his first semester at college. This was not in his plans. I was touched and moved, so I waited and prayed about it a while longer. We continued to discuss the option. Finally, in early September 2004, I broached the subject with my immediate supervisor. He was in the process of leaving for a new assignment, so I would have to wait and ask my new supervisor. When my new supervisor arrived, he agreed to support me, but he wanted me to wait until he got settled. So, I had to wait longer, while I identified who would take over my duties while I was gone. There are no replacements if an active-duty individual deploys, merely a gap in the workforce. I worked with him to identify a replacement and chose one of the most competent men who worked for me, a retired Lieutenant Colonel, who was now a DA Civilian. He was heading the Plans section and was a perfect choice. He would do as good a job as I did, if not better. He was quiet, but hard-working and willing to tackle any task and work it to completion.

Next, I had to check with the G-2 and get his approval. When I told him my reasons, he was supportive and made some inquiries into openings for O-6s in Iraq. By late October, it looked like a slot had been identified heading the Intel

Analysis Center at Camp Victory, Baghdad. I was excited, but I could do nothing until I received my orders. A week, two weeks went by; all the while I was calling the deployment folks, calling Iraq and trying to find out what the problem was with my orders. It seems there was a glitch in the system and the position I was going to was already filled. I was devastated. I had prayed, anguished, and contemplated about this for so long, and I faithfully believed it was God's will for me to go, only to have it fall through. Well, I reasoned, maybe the boys needed me to be home; maybe I had some purpose here. So, I accepted it and settled back to work as usual.

Around this time, I had decided to sell my home in Woodbridge and buy a condo near the Pentagon, eliminating the hour commute back and forth to work every day. I finally found a place and closed on a condo in early December. Well, I had recently moved in and started to get settled and ready for Christmas, when I got THE call. I was being deployed to Iraq to command the Joint Interrogation and Debriefing Center at Abu Ghraib. It was the 20th of December, and I was scheduled to depart on January 2, leaving me about two weeks to prepare to leave.

When I got the call, I was on my way to meet the boys to go Christmas shopping, so I continued to the mall, met with the boys, hugged them, and told them I was deploying to Iraq. I don't remember doing much shopping, as we each processed what this meant and how it would impact each of our lives. At least Joe was settled in school and already had friends and a support system there. But arrangements would have to be made for Frank who was finishing his senior year of high school online and did most of his learning via classes on the computer. I decided for my daughter-in-law, Eva's, brother Alex who taught high school in DC to come and live in my new condo, oversee Frank, and take care of my home while I was gone. I turned over responsibilities to my replacement at work, and briefed him on the status of projects, issues, and responsibilities.

We decided to go to Buffalo for Christmas, so I could tell my family. The holidays in Buffalo were full of love and support, until my family found out I volunteered to go. Why would I do this? We came back home to DC for New Year's Eve, and I had a quiet celebration with a couple who were dear friends of mine, but the mood was somber, and we were all counting the minutes till midnight so they could leave and I could go to bed.

Finally, January 2, 2005, arrived, and Joe and Frank took me to the airport to see me off. I will never forget the picture of these two man-boys standing there together, crying and watching their mom go off to war. This picture is forever etched in my mind and heart.

18

Iraq: We're Not in Kansas Anymore

Iraq was terrifying. Terrorists and Saddam's Former Regime members continually attacked American and Allied forces. I was a Colonel, and I was going to command in a warzone. I had to be trained and ready. So, my first stop was Fort Bliss, Texas for my pre-deployment training. The first couple days were spent getting our equipment and gear: two large duffle bags full of desert uniforms, body armor, helmets, and gas masks. This was followed by weapons qualification, cultural briefings on Iraq, Rules of Engagement (ROE), the Geneva Conventions, and training to prepare us for attacks in our vehicles, in convoys, and what to do if captured. We had to complete the administrative aspects: physicals, updating medical records, making sure our pay documents were in order and our wills were completed. Every day made the gravity of what we were about to embark on a reality.

Finally, training was over, and we were getting a 4-day pass before heading out. All of a sudden, 14 of us were singled out and told we were departing in two days, on a special flight, because we were urgently needed in our new assignments. Frank decided to come and see me for the 4-day pass, but when it was canceled, he still decided to come and spend a day and a half with me. As it turned out, the day he arrived, I was sick with some kind of flu. I spent the day sleeping, while he played video games in the hotel room. Finally he begged, "Can we please get something to eat?" I dragged myself out of bed and we went out for dinner and a movie. It must have impacted him as he reminded me not long ago the movie was "Spanglish." This time together made an impact on him and on me as well. I was so grateful to have a member of my family with me as I departed for the unknown. We ended up having a close, comforting evening. The next day, we drove to the airport together, said our good-byes, and he flew back to DC, and I flew on to Kuwait, my first stop on my way to Iraq.

Our group, "the Super 14" as we were nicknamed, was treated exceptionally well at the military base in Kuwait, which could be likened to a vacation resort: swimming pools, a club, a theater, and plenty of shopping. But we never enjoyed this as we were quickly rushed onto the plane taking us to the military airfield in Baghdad.

We flew into the airfield at night. There were no runway lights, and the shades were all drawn on our tiny plane's windows. We deplaned and boarded a bus, whose windows were also shaded, and were taken to Camp Victory and our quarters for the night. The next day we would meet members of our new units. I awoke the next morning and went to breakfast. I was surprised how good the mess hall food was there and enjoyed a big breakfast. Halfway through the breakfast, a siren sounded, and everyone hit the ground. There were incoming rockets, but shortly thereafter, it was called all clear and normal activities were resumed. Welcome to Iraq.

I was driven to Task Force 34 (TF34) Headquarters and met my boss, MG Brandenburg. After meeting him and talking for a short time, I met some of the other staff, and I met my First Sergeant, who was escorting me to Abu Ghraib where I would be living. As I looked around Camp Victory, a section of Iraq outside Baghdad, I saw a beautiful part of the country. There were paved streets, and much of the land was graveled, not dusty desert. Plus, there were palm trees and vegetation.

The Aw Faw Palace was where Saddam Hussein once lived. His lieutenants' homes surrounded his palace. All the homes were beautiful and centered around a lake. Now, American Forces, along with British, Australian, Polish, Spanish, and other Coalition Allies, occupied the buildings. "I can do this. This does not look so bad." Officers and NCOs had their own trailers, and some of the Colonels had their own indoor plumbing. Additionally, Camp Victory was well reinforced at this point, so body armor was not required, and many folks could be seen exercising and running in PT gear. They had a movie theater, a couple mess halls, and a post exchange (PX—a military version of Wal-Mart); it was a beautiful area. I was reassured already.

Top, my First Sergeant, led me to the convoy heading out to Abu Ghraib. We shared a little about each other, and I quickly knew he was someone I could count on. We had the most disturbing conversation. Top told me, "You know, ma'am, Saddam has a $50K price on the heads of Colonels which would likely be doubled for a FEMALE Colonel. You could be worth $100K to some lucky Iraqi who captured you." A shiver went up my spine. In a weird way, it made me feel important. It also gave me a sense of terror I have never experienced. The implications of being captured became all too real. Top continued, "My primary job is to make sure you don't get captured and to keep you alive." This sounded good to me. Top had my back. He gave me his loyalty because of his training and integrity; but I knew I would have to earn his respect.

We headed over to get our pre-convoy briefing and found this to be the procedure every time we went on a convoy in Iraq. The briefing covered what to do if we were attacked or surrounded and what to do if we were captured. We were told to put on our body armor, as well as helmets, and to lock and load our weapons. This was not a classroom exercise; this was Iraq. This was real.

This first convoy trip to Abu Ghraib was terrifying. Even though it was winter, it was in the high 90s during the day. I was sweating profusely. I was outfitted in full body armor and my weapon was in the ready position. The trip was about 20 miles, taking what seemed to be hours, as the convoy wound its way through some dangerous Iraqi territory, towns where many of Saddam's loyal followers were living, and I learned they regularly attacked the convoys. I was terrified for the whole trip. My knuckles were white from holding on to my seat and my heart was pounding; I am sure my eyes were as big as saucers and my apprehension was palpable. Finally, we arrived at Abu Ghraib.

Abu Ghraib was where Saddam sent anyone who disobeyed or even disagreed with him or someone he simply did not like. There were cells where he kept groups of prisoners and each cell had a large hook hanging from the ceiling, used to hang someone on the spot. His "death chamber" where his executions were held was here as well.

Originally, the US forces were in tents surrounding the compound, and the detainees were in the cells. Since they were attacked on a regular basis, after a short time, the US reasoned, "What's wrong with this picture?" and put the detainees in tents, and they took over the hard facilities.

Top showed me around, took me to my office area, where I met some of my staff, and I talked to them briefly. At last, Top showed me to my quarters. My "hooch" was one of the cells I mentioned earlier. I had a bed and a cupboard and a couple drawers for my belongings. It became obvious I shared my hooch with a couple mice. Over my bed was one of the hooks Saddam used to hang people. Every night I went to sleep looking. "How many men had been hung from this hook?" This ever-present reminder of death, as well as the lack of vegetation, the dryness of the land, the starkness of the cement structures surrounded by concertina wire, created a dark gloom in Abu Ghraib. The evil lurking there penetrated my being.

Finally, I was alone in my hooch at Abu Ghraib, Iraq. I looked around. I was devastated. I was overwhelmed with a sense of despair. I set some sage on fire. Sage was given to me by a friend to rid the space of darkness and any evil lurking there. As the smoke spread throughout the room, I cried and prayed. I sobbed and desperately pleaded, "Oh God, this is way worse than I imagined it would be. This is too much, way more than I can handle. I can't do this. I am way over my head." How could I let myself get into this position? What was a mother of five doing here in a combat zone? How did I get here? Why was I here? Is this how an Army Colonel, recently sent to command the Joint Interrogation and Debriefing Center at Abu Ghraib should be feeling?

But interestingly, after about an hour of crying, despairing, and praying, this sense of peace came over me, and I knew I would not be put into any situation unless I had the strength to handle it. I didn't need to worry. A couple days later, I knew it was a blessing to be assigned here and, for whatever reason, Abu Ghraib was where I was meant to be.

When I was deployed, I took it seriously. I had to focus on the issues at hand; my life and the lives of the military members, who worked for me, may depend on it. It was harder for my loved ones at home, especially my children, because they did not know what was going on. For me, I had a certain adrenaline rush and a kind of excitement, combined with fear of the unknown. My loved ones simply had worry and fear. I believe it was helpful to them for me to call periodically and send emails daily. I sent missives, telling them stories of what was going on. I hoped this quelled their fears and anxieties. It also provided me comfort and an escape from what was my new "normal." It was grounding, but almost surreal to hear what was going on back home. It grounded me to hear everyone was going about their business and living their lives; however, it was surreal to see how different life was in the States from the lives of the people here in Iraq

Due to the history of Abu Ghraib as Saddam's death camp and its proximity to insurgent villages, we were always on alert. Everyone was required to wear body armor, helmets, and weapons, unless in their immediate work area. This meant you wore your protective gear every time you went to the mess hall or visited the latrine, showers, or any place on the compound. The showers were in outdoor sheds. There was no indoor plumbing, and we had to use a porta-potty. One of the worst assaults on my senses was to go to a porta-potty which had been sitting in 130-degree temperatures all day. I would take a deep breath and try to hold it until I was done. The Mess Hall was not bad, pretty good meals, except for the occasional weeks when they could not get fresh fruits and vegetables.

The military staff at Abu Ghraib was a hardworking lot. There was an O-5 who had been in charge temporarily, from the time my predecessor left until I arrived (about 3 weeks). He was an AF Lieutenant Colonel and a good man. The unit was composed of Individual Augmentees who came from various units. There was a collection of Marines, Navy, Air Force, and Army assigned there. The unit had about half of the allotted slots filled, and they were doing their best to keep things running. Many of them had not had a day off in a month and were working 14 to 16 hours a day on a regular basis.

A couple months into my tour, the people comprising my unit (Individual Augmentees) were augmented with an Interrogation unit out of Korea. Our numbers doubled. Unfortunately, so did our problems and challenges.

There was a lot of bravado in the new unit. Many members acted as if they were better than the Individual Augmentees, who had been working long hours with little to no days off. The unit from Korea had some hardworking, effective members, but some not so productive. Prior to this unit arriving, I had a young marine, an E-5, who was almost single-handedly running the Intelligence Control Element (ICE). He was smart, hardworking, and efficient. He was producing many Intelligence reports, as well as providing papers delineating suggestions for even more efficiency in the compilation of Intelligence reports and cross-indexing the volumes of intelligence coming from various sources throughout Iraq. A Major, an E-7 and two E-5's replaced him, but this team did not perform to the levels of the lone Marine. These instances obviously caused friction between the two groups of people comprising the unit.

Also, the Battalion Commander (a lieutenant colonel whom I will call LTC Brownnose) anticipated HE would be the commander of the JIDC, and instead he found himself as an executive officer (XO) to a female colonel—ME. He was not a happy camper, yet he was sweet as sugar when he talked to me. LTC Brownnose would always tell me what I wanted to hear. However, I wanted to hear straight talk and the truth. That's why this was an especially challenging relationship.

19

Abu Ghraib: Life as Usual

After the unlawful interrogation practices reported in the news in early 2004, Task Force (TF) 134 took over the running of the compound at Abu Ghraib and we all came under MG Brandenburg, the TF Commander. There were two other colonels (O-6s) beside me at Abu Ghraib: The Commander of the Hospital and the Post Commander who was in charge of the facilities (mess hall, laundry, offices) and security of the Post. Security included the Marine unit guarding the outer perimeter and the Military Police (MP) protecting the interior. The MPs also had responsibility for the care and feeding of the detainees. The Joint Interrogation and Debriefing Center (JIDC) was another unit at Abu Ghraib. Additionally, there was one other element, not connected to the US Forces located there. There was a prison, where citizens who had broken Iraqi laws, been tried, convicted, and sentenced in Iraqi courts, were serving out their term. Some of these were real hardened criminals (murderers and thieves). Iraqi prison guards supervised and were responsible for this group. The prison was on the other side of the JIDC offices; even though the buildings were made of cinder blocks, I could hear the prisoners on the other side of my office wall. Creepy.

I learned a lot about the Iraqi people during my time in Iraq. Iraqis generally do not trust institutional power and they expect physical abuse when detained. When one studies the history of the Iraqi people, Iraq has been occupied by non-Iraqis throughout the years—from the Persians to the Mongols to the Ottoman occupation. And the Iraqis have never been treated well by the occupiers. We wanted to change this. By the time I left Iraq at the end of 2005, the per capita income had doubled since 2003; there were five times as many cars and phones; there were 32 times more internet users; and independent media went from zero to 44 television stations, 72 radio stations, and 100 newspapers.

US Forces conducted raids on buildings suspected of housing terrorists, kidnappers, and murderers, or people suspected of bombings, improvised explosive devices (IEDs), or vehicle borne improvised explosive devices (VBIED). When soldiers burst into Iraqi homes in the middle of the night, they were relieved we didn't kill them. Persons of interest and people involved in attacks would be brought to Abu Ghraib and detained for questioning, so referred to as detainees.

When detainees were brought to Abu Ghraib, various representatives from the Post in-processed them. First, a unit assigned to the Post Commander de-loused them, gave them a shower and clean clothes—a yellow jumpsuit. They gave them a copy of the Koran (or in some cases a Bible) and a prayer mat. They gave them cots to sleep on, three meals a day, books to read, daily exercise time, and showers three times a week. A hospital team gave them a physical, and if they had any medical conditions needing to be treated, they would receive treatment. Representatives from the Joint Interrogation and Debriefing Center (JIDC) compiled a series of questions for the detainees. If they were identified as having potential intelligence value, they would be scheduled for interrogations.

The detainees had visitation privileges and friends and relatives were allowed to visit twice a week. The MPs had to inspect all visitors coming in, as they often found knives in the soles of their sandals, as well as other weapons hidden on their person. Visitation served a dual purpose. We could track the contacts and connections of the detainees we knew were members of the Former Regime. Secondly, friends and families could see their loved ones were not being abused. In fact, between the health care and the regular meals, within a month most of the detainees were healthier than when they had arrived.

The culture was, as expected, dissimilar from what I was used to, but in other ways was surprisingly relatable, most notably the relationships between families and friends. These were people like you and me—teachers and businesspeople, engineers, and hairdressers. I could relate to the people who had dogs and kids, birthday parties and family get-togethers. The surreal part was the reality of what these people had to deal with daily, starting with a cruel dictator like Saddam. Since Saddam was overthrown, they had to adjust to a government dealing with the differences between rival factions and striving to restore order. They were also dealing with remnants of Saddam's regime, which were fighting against the allied forces, including the US. Here I was, in the middle of all this.

During my time in Iraq, the US continued to put money into new and existing Iraqi facilities, even as we provided plans for the US to transfer control to the Iraqi government. There was a political push back in 2005 for the US to get out of the detainee operations business by the end of the year. However (in my opinion), the Iraqi political infrastructure was not strong enough or structured enough to assume those responsibilities. We were moving toward this end. We were training prison guards. We were teaching international standards for maintenance of prisoners. Impacting my command directly, we started working with Iraqi interrogators to teach them the same guidelines we were using for interrogations—those making us a gentler, kinder army. But we were not there yet.

The geography of the land had its share of beauty as well

as challenges. Abu Ghraib was all desert; there was no vegeta-tion, as there was at Camp Victory, no paved roads, only sand everywhere. When the wind blew, which it often did, it blew the sand all over. Sand got into everything: my ears, my eyes, and any crevice on my body. When I returned to my hooch at night, the sand had blown under the door, about five feet into the room. I used to place a big plastic sheet over my bed, to keep sand off my blankets and pillows. When I came in at night, I took the plastic off and crawled into bed. I would put the plastic back on when I awoke in the morning. My hooch was not a place where I wanted to hang out and relax; the only time I was there was to sleep.

When it rained, the sand did not soak up the water; the water sat on top of the ground and formed this thick muck that stuck to everything. I arrived in winter, which is the rainy season, and it would get cool when the sun set, but rose to about 50 degrees when the sun was high. Once summer came, we experienced the real heat—sometimes as high as 130 de-grees during the day. I sometimes had to change my t-shirt (which was worn under my desert uniform) a couple times a day. The sweat was pouring down my back. Consequently, we constantly had to hydrate, and we emphasized this to every-one. We had cases of water everywhere.

I had never seen a sandstorm before coming to Iraq. The sandstorms here in the desert were horrible. Imagine a fog hanging over your town. But it wasn't condensation and moisture. It was sand. It got into your eyes, your ears, and your mouth if you tried to talk. And it sat there, sometimes for days at a time. During the few times the sun shined, coming through the fog, it colored everything orange. It was so eerie.

The first day I rode in the convoy coming from Camp Vic-tory, I was terrified. Shortly after I arrived, MG Brandenburg decided he wanted weekly staff meetings at his office at Camp Victory. Every week I would be taking this horrible convoy ride to Camp Victory and back. The first couple times I was as terrified as ever, but over time, the terrifying became normal, and it wasn't long before I even dozed off on the way there.

On the way to Camp Victory, we passed farmland, where we could see families working in the fields. The troops in the convoy threw candy to the Iraqi kids who stood out there and waved anytime we passed. They are not any different than the US kids when it comes to candy. Sometimes, we would see a group of young boys/men playing soccer on a cleared-out piece of land. This place, this war was their reality. Life goes on.

Occasionally, I would go into Camp Victory on a Friday for a meeting or teleconference. We often had guest speakers who would give briefings on their expertise. One individual was a finance guy who tracked the money sources of terrorists. Like many criminals, drugs were a big source of revenue. They would use new cars to smuggle the drugs in and out of the country. Houda, a female Iraqi terrorist, had a few car dealerships spread throughout Iraq she used to facilitate this endeavor.

Another unit I visited on Camp Victory was the Counter-Improvised Explosive Devices (IED) Exploitation Center (CEXC—the acronym was pronounced SEXY.) They had a team who would go out to the site of IEDs and VBIEDs (vehicle-borne) and study the ruins to determine the way the devices were made, materials used, and detonation triggers. Ironically, once this team started studying them, it was discovered the Iraqis often went back to the same site to set off another IED. By tracking them, the CEXC was able to prevent repeats at the same site, until the Iraqis got wise to them. A friend of mine headed the CEXC, so we were able to work together and share information he learned from his team, and we learned from interrogations. The whole idea was to save lives—Iraqi and US.

One Saturday morning after a Friday night at Camp Victory, I left the Mess Hall and started walking to TF 134 HQ. I had all my gear from the convoy the night before, including my rucksack, containing my overnight necessities and body armor and helmet. As always, I had my weapon in my pistol belt at my side. A couple young Marines saw me, lugging all my stuff, and offered me a ride. Gratefully I accepted. We exchanged some small talk, and I found out they were part of the general's security detail. They dropped me off, I thanked them, and I went into TF 134 Headquarters. I am embarrassed and humiliated at what happened next. As soon as I arrived, I was hit with the sudden realization I did not have my weapon! My issued holster must have been a little worn and a little loose, and my 9mm slipped out of the holster in the car. It never occurred to me that my issued equipment was not good enough. Anyone who knows ANYTHING knows you never lose control or possession of your weapon. And here I was without mine. I lost possession in a foreign land. The consequences could be disastrous.

I went to Top and told him. I gave him all the info I had on the Marines. Reflecting back, I did remember hearing "clank" at some point on the ride to my meeting, but I assumed it was something in the trunk. It must have been my weapon falling out. I had no doubt my weapon was in their vehicle, but they were driving the same navy-blue sedan every officer and unit on Camp Victory was issued. Top said he would take care of it. The first thing he did was to go to the Marine Gunnery Sergeant assigned to TF 134. He happened to be talking to the Navy Senior Chief Petty Officer, so the three of them took on the mission to find my weapon.

I was sweating bullets all day hoping and praying my weapon would be found. Not only would there be repercussions for me (a lengthy investigation would ensue to determine the extent of my responsibility) but a US weapon in the hands of an Iraqi could result in a myriad of crimes or worse. The team kept reporting back to me. They went to the Marine Corps (MC) unit stationed at Camp Victory, but after canvasing all the troops, nothing. They located the security detail of the MC general on Post and found there was a big meeting, with about six MC generals visiting there, all with their own security details. So, this group of three senior enlisted men set out to locate the security details of all six generals. It was getting late in the day, and I would have to start preparing to convoy home soon. But there was no way I was going back to Abu Ghraib without my weapon, and I wasn't about to confess to my boss yet.

The group continued looking and finally they found the Marines who had given me the ride. The problem was, they had recently taken their car over to the motor pool to have it washed. One of them went with Top and his team to identify their car, but as they got there, it was about to enter the cleaning area. The Gunnery gallantly leapt over the barrier and stopped the guy seconds before he opened the door. The significance of this is the laborers at the carwash at the motor pool were Iraqis. What would have happened if THEY found the pistol? I fear no one would ever see my weapon again.

I owed a debt to these three service members. Maybe the general would have excused me. Maybe this neglect would not have impacted my career. But it could also have had serious repercussions. I could have been charged; a US Army weapon could have ended in the wrong hands. The potential for disastrous results was enormous. All of this weighed on my mind, and I was filled with gratitude. Did these three professional military men go to great lengths because of their own sense of responsibility, or did they extend themselves because I had earned their respect? I know the former was true; I also hope the latter. I went to Top and trusted him and the Gunnery Sergeant and the Senior Chief Petty Officer. If anyone could find my weapon, I knew these three could. I respected their ability and their dedication. They did not disappoint. I was keenly aware there was no way I could ever repay these three men. I wrote a letter of commendation for each of them. But this only pales in comparison to how they went above and beyond the call of duty to save my ass. I learned many lessons about leadership that day. Leaders still make mistakes, sometimes huge mistakes. We do not have the luxury to be careless. I also learned to trust and respect the capabilities of non-commissioned officers. They are leaders. The last lesson I learned was to test my own equipment and make sure it works. If I had a gas mask and I never tested, it could have proved fatal if I discovered a leak in a gas attack. Immediately I bought a beautiful, new, leather holster, which held my pistol tightly and securely. It would NEVER get away from me again.

I had hoped to bring some healing and comfort to the military men and women deployed to Iraq. I personally found comfort in practicing my faith. There was a shortage of Catholic priests in Iraq, not enough to cover all the Sunday Masses throughout the country. So, a priest visited Abu Ghraib on Thursdays for our weekly Sunday Mass. This was not ideal, but we learned to accept it. However, when Easter Sunday approached, Thursday Mass would not suffice. According to church history, Easter Sunday represents the resurrection, after Christ had been crucified on Good Friday. Easter services on Thursday simply would not do. I contacted the Chief of Chaplains in Iraq, who turned out to be the same Post Chaplain I had at the AWC. I called him regularly and told him my soldiers needed and deserved to have services here on Easter more than other locations, surely more than the folks who had the comfortable existence at Camp Victory. We already missed out on USO Shows, because it was "too dangerous" for celebrities to travel to Abu Ghraib. I bugged him and begged him until finally he called to tell me he had a priest to say Mass on Easter at Abu Ghraib, but I needed to make travel arrangements for him. I immediately called the general (who flew out to Abu Ghraib for Sunday meetings) and he agreed to let the chaplain fly out with him. So, on Easter Sunday, we had a priest at Abu Ghraib to say Mass. This was a small but significant comfort to the Catholics and other Christians stationed there. I also believe it brought some semblance of home and normalcy; we were able to observe a holiday in the same manner and time as our loved ones back home.

This was a volatile time in Iraq. There were attacks all over. Convoys were hit and ambushed. Units came under fire. It was Saturday, April 2, 2005. I had gone to my regular staff meeting at Camp Victory in the morning. I came back to Abu Ghraib and was in the Mess Hall having dinner with the Post Commander and the Hospital Commander and a couple NCOs from our units. We were nearing the end of our meal when we heard a blast. We were all stunned and stared at one another. Within a split second, another blast followed, and we all jumped to don our body armor and helmets. We were under attack! As the rockets were shot inside our compound, the walls vibrated and shook inside the dining facility. If you have ever seen a war movie in a theater with surround sound, you have a glimpse of the sound and the encompassing terror. The post commander radioed the perimeter security force. For two and a half hours, Abu Ghraib was under attack (Al Qaeda in Iraq later claimed credit for the attack). We were being hit with rockets and mortars, as well as machine guns. The first thing was to secure the people in the dining facility; many were civilians and contractors and not prepared for combat. We immediately had them lie under the tables, so they would have some protection from incoming blasts and debris. I have to admit at first, I was disoriented, stunned, and afraid. We were being targeted. I became concerned about my folks at the unit, as well as those in billeting near the perimeter. I can't say I was not terrified but stepping into my role and focusing on my job as Commander and my unit personnel helped to distract me from the terror of the moment. The Post Commander and I were in communication, and he kept me informed. A vehicle-borne improvised explosive device (VBIED) was set off near the tower on the perimeter. The outside wall was breached but the MPs were able to keep them from penetrating. Some of the detainees rioted and started a fire with rags wrapped around a tent pole. This occurred near the breach of the outside wall, but again US forces within the compound were able to squelch the attack and keep the detainees under control.

I got an MP to drive me back to the unit to check on my personnel, assess damages, and report to MG Brandenburg. There were holes in the walls of the JIDC buildings and near the interrogation areas, but no one was injured. When I got through to the general, he told me there was some artillery coverage on the way, but we later found out they were fired on and had to return before arriving at Abu Ghraib. When it was finally over and things started to quiet, we took a head count of unit personnel and assessed damages. The only injuries were to four MC personnel who were guarding the outer perimeter. I was able to get on my computer and I already had a message from a couple people back home, asking if I was okay. It never occurred to me that anyone back in the States would have any idea of this attack, but I quickly contacted my kids and let them know I was safe.

Hindsight is great. Looking back, we found an extraordinary number of prison guards (from the Iraqi prison on the compound) had reported off or simply left early. Also, Al Jazeera television station in Iraq was filming the whole attack. Coincidence? I think not. Additionally, we allowed an Iraqi radio station to broadcast to the detainees for two hours each day. We later found out the detainees were warned to take cover as well as to seize any opportunity to gain control when the fighting commenced. This was further evidence it was a well-planned and coordinated attack. Except for the four Marines, our casualties were minor, and they were treated at the hospital. Reports of Iraqi fatalities ranged between 60-80. I admire the marines and soldiers who defended our perimeter. And I am so proud of all the JIDC members who defended their position after the enemy breached our wall. This was an instance when the augmentees as well as the unit from Korea worked together with a common goal. They were well trained and did an exemplary job. This was the only time I was directly involved in an attack during my time at Abu Ghraib. Yes, Iraq was indeed a terrifying place, and for this short time, it was my home.

20

JIDC: Organization and Mission

Who is Private First Class (PFC) Maupin? Why did I care about him? Shortly after arriving in Iraq, I heard the story of Private First Class (PFC) Maupin. He was a soldier who was on a convoy attacked by the Iraqis on April 9, 2004. PFC Maupin, another soldier, and a contractor were captured. The contractor escaped, and the other soldier was murdered, his body recovered a few days later. PFC Maupin may have been murdered but until the body was found, he was listed as missing in action (MIA) and his unit continued to look for him, dead or alive. They searched extensively after he was attacked. Soon, they fulfilled their deployment requirements and rotated back to the US. A group of MPs continued the search but to no avail. There was a lot of conflicting information being collected by the various units looking for PFC Maupin. Some folks believed he was still alive, and he was kept prisoner somewhere. Al Jazeera (Iraqi television station) had a tape of him being made to kneel by a hole and being shot in the head. However, the picture was grainy, and he could not be identified with certainty.

We never leave one of our own in enemy territory. I put together a team in my analysis section who compiled all the information they could on the convoy and PFC Maupin; this became their primary focus. The additional personnel from the unit supplementing the JIDC made this possible. They developed line diagrams, connecting information on people connected to the attack on the convoy. They looked at possible places he might have been held as well as places he might have been buried. We brought in Iraqis who might have information on him, and we developed interrogation plans to question these folks. We kept adding information, getting closer and closer to the location of PFC Maupin. Because he was MIA, he continued to be paid—his paycheck going home to his wife and new baby. He also continued to be promoted. As more and more time passed, more units tried to find him, and became frustrated when they kept hitting dead ends. Our team at Abu Ghraib became the primary source of reliable information on PFC Maupin in Iraq.

I wish I could tell you we found PFC Maupin before I left, but we did not. We came optimistically close. We were pretty sure this one Iraqi knew where he was buried, but he was not talking. Luckily, we brought in his son on a raid. We used his son to try to leverage his father to come in and talk to us. We were so sure our plan was working, our behavioral science team helped develop an Interrogation Plan. Knowing how important family was to many Iraqis and to this man, we would talk to him about family and the loyalty of a father to a son, how a father would do anything for his son, to protect him, keep him safe, bring him home. We would show him a picture of his son. And a picture of PFC Maupin. We would use his connection to his son to relate to PFC Maupin's father and his desire to bring him home. We offered to release his son in return for information on PFC Maupin. Unfortunately, he took the letter we had sent him and went to another US unit he had contacts with, and they kept him for questioning on another matter, and he was never released and able to provide us the information we needed. It was terribly upsetting to all of us who had put so much time and effort into "working" this Iraqi. We were so close, and another unit blew it for us. Perhaps unintentionally, but, nonetheless, we were under different commands, different missions. We found out, but it was too late; we had lost our opportunity.

Another initiative to find PFC Maupin was to bring in some cadaver dogs; we had narrowed his possible burial place to a couple sites, but they were in the proximity of some dangerous Iraqi neighborhoods. We arranged to bring in some specialized dogs to find the body, but they only had a small window of time during which they had some coverage and security. The team with the dogs was working for about an hour when they started getting heavy enemy fire and they had to abort the mission before the dogs could find anything.

During all this time, Maupin's family was holding out hope he was still alive. His mom wanted to know if we drew a composite photo, showing him with facial hair and long hair, and if we were looking for him in neighboring countries in case he had escaped and made it to a surrounding country. His mother sent a detailed letter to General Casey with several questions she wanted answered. MG Brandenburg sent it to me to read. I also read the response someone in Gen. Casey's office had put together. I couldn't sleep. I woke in the middle of the night and knew I needed to respond. I told MG Brandenburg the response was too impersonal and sounded like someone was answering an essay question on a history exam. This was a mother who wanted information on her child who had been captured by an enemy. The response needed to be sensitive to the situation and I re-worded a portion of the letter as an example. The next day, MG Brandenburg called me. He agreed with me, and he sent my re-work of the letter to Gen. Casey. I found out later the portion of the letter I put together was sent to Maupin's mom. However, this brought me no sense of pride or accomplishment. Her son was still out there, and he still was not found. I had a silver band with PFC Maupin's name, rank, and date of his capture, which I wore until he was found, which finally happened in 2008. PFC Maupin had been promoted multiple times and was now SSG Maupin. Four years after his capture, his body was finally found and was sent home to his family. I believe the information we collected, as part of our mission at the JIDC, was instrumental in finally helping to find him and bring SSG Maupin home.

I established another section during my time in Iraq which proved to be a terrific source of intelligence. Two amazing soldiers from the Korean unit, an E-7 and an E-8 came to me one day and briefed a plan to form a Counterintelligence Collection team. They proposed a vehicle for any Iraqis who had information and wanted to help us, to do so anonymously. They were convincing and knowledgeable, and their procedures provided safety for any Iraqis wishing to help us. They were seeking Iraqis to act as informants for us. After a series of discussions and pitching it to the General, the Abu Ghraib Field Counterintelligence Office (AFCO) was established. It became extremely successful. One of their informants was in the employ of a member of Saddam's regime. I'll call his employer Abdul. This young man saw his parents murdered by Abdul and he was forced to work for him. His main objective was to get enough money from giving us information to take his sisters to a safe place to live. During the time he was working with us, he provided locations for three secret hiding places for hundreds of Iraqi weapons, as well as information on meetings his boss was having with other known and wanted Iraqis. One week, our informant did not show on the designated day. Or the next. Finally, almost two weeks later, he came in, with slashes on his back from beatings and three fingernails missing from his hands. Abdul suspected someone in his employ was passing information and proceeded to torture a group of them to find out whom. This young man did not cave; he came back more determined than ever to help the coalition forces apprehend his boss, collect the reward, and move with his sisters to a safer place. This determination and love and responsibility towards family were so evident in many of the Iraqis we met.

We did not have the resources ourselves to arrange an ambush to get his boss, so we had to rely on another operations unit in the country. The first time our informant told us a time and place to find Abdul the operations unit was there, but they didn't do anything, because they wanted to verify the reliability of the information. The informant was devastated, but hung in there until he had another chance. A couple months later, another opportunity to catch Abdul was presented to us, and we again coordinated with the operations unit to apprehend him. This informant put himself in jeopardy every time he gave us information. He badly wanted the reward for the capture of his boss, because it was substantial enough to give him and his sisters a good start somewhere else. The Operations unit again failed; they were called out on another mission. After all the information the informant had provided, we again failed him. The meager funds we were able to give him did not compensate for the risks he was taking. We never saw him again after the last incident and lost the opportunity to capture Abdul.

Each section at the JIDC played a vital role in supporting our interrogation mission. There were the administrative and logistics sections, each taking care of the soldier's needs (pay, promotions, awards, feeding, housing). There was a JAG Office, which advised on legal issues and insured Interrogation plans and methods used were legal. They were also a legal resource to the people of the unit for personal as well as professional matters. There was a Behavioral Scientist Consultation Team (BSCT), which provided insights to addressing behaviors of the detainees and provided the interrogators with tools they did not learn at school. These tools empowered the interrogators to obtain reliable information they could not have learned through deprivation or torture. We had a medical unit that examined each detainee before and after an interrogation, looking for evidence of abuse either in the compound before the interrogation, or during the interrogation. Finally, there was the Intelligence Control Element (ICE), which compiled information gathered during interrogations and converted it to Intelligence Information Reports (IIRs).

There was a group of contractors working for me who I had a great amount of respect for—our translators. Often during interrogations there was the potential to uncover sensitive and classified information, therefore our translators had to have a Top Secret (TS) Clearance. The first requirement for a TS clearance was citizenship; they had to be US Citizens. Since it would take years to teach the language to military members, the Army hired contractors who were Iraqi and already US citizens. Security background investigations were conducted on them before hiring them as contractors. Some people sneered, saying the contractors were doing it for the money, but I wholeheartedly disagree. These people not only put themselves in jeopardy by leaving their safe American homes and families to come to Iraq and assist us, but many of them had family members in Iraq who would also be in danger if they were found out. This group of US citizens believed in what we were doing enough to take this risk and come to Iraq and work for the US military as translators. I admired and respected them.

21

Interrogation: A More Humane Approach

When people hear "interrogations" they conjure images of waterboarding, food and sensory deprivation, and torture. I came to the JIDC hoping to change this image. I was the first long-term Commander to live at Abu Ghraib. There was an interim commander before me, but he was only there for a couple months. I heard he slept with his pistol cocked on the table next to his bed, and once he knew I was on the way, he left, not wanting to stay even a couple weeks longer to do a change over with me. I am thankful for the resolution I had on my first night at Abu Ghraib, when I worried this place was too much for me to deal with. The peace I acquired on my first night served me well for the rest of my tour. I fortunately did not worry on a day-to-day basis about my safety.

We were brought in to ensure the Geneva Conventions were enforced during interrogations. If you've ever read the Geneva Conventions, they are extremely vague: for example, it prohibits "cruel treatment and torture." However, restrictions were not spelled out, leaving it open to interpretation. What constitutes cruel treatment? Food deprivation? For how long? Sleep deprivation? To what extent? At what point does someone cross the line? So, stronger, more defined measures needed to be put in place and enforced. We worked with MG Brandenburg to delineate and enforce specific restrictions.

It should be noted Saddam's Iraq did not comply with the Geneva Conventions, not even for his own people. We know his soldiers tortured and killed American soldiers who were captured.

The incidents happening at Abu Ghraib in early 2004 were in the news. Soldiers at Abu Ghraib used unlawful interrogation methods. These soldiers were military police (MP), not military intelligence (MI). The problem with this was the MPs oversaw the feeding and care of the men who were detained. These detainees were involved in attacks, or they were notorious members of the Former Regime. The MPs overseeing them were yelled at and spit upon by some of the detainees; some detainees urinated on them or threw feces at them. It was impossible to be in the position of keeping order among these people during the day and also be the same people questioning and interrogating them. The MPs were interrogating with mindsets and prejudices established through their dealings with the detainees daily. In my opinion, they lacked the clarity, distance, and focus needed for effective interrogations. And they were young and there was no on-site leadership overseeing the process. This was a recipe for disaster.

MG Brandenburg and his subordinate units (including the JIDC) in TF 134 changed all this, and we put measures in place so no abuse of any kind would happen again. A clear separation was established between the soldiers who oversaw the care and feeding of the detainees (the military police—MPs) and those who did the interrogations (military intelligence—MI); the MPs would sign the detainee over to the Interrogator, so there was a paper trail for each detainee. The medical team assigned was not under my command (to avoid any pressure to cover-up any findings) and they would physically examine all detainees, prior to interrogation, as well as afterwards, looking for any signs of abuse, either before or during interrogations. Of course, the JIDC still worked with the MPs to improve the process. Even though there was a clear separation between the MPs and the Interrogators, the MPs still shared useful information with us, such as identifying to us the "leaders" in the compound or those with skills outside of ordinary farming. For example, the MPs often found weapons being made from pieces of metal fencing, or simple explosives with whatever the detainees could find or have smuggled in.

Upon in-processing of the detainees, an interrogator would ask some basic questions in order to determine whether he had any information of intelligence value. If so, the interrogator would put together an Interrogation Plan which was reviewed by his first line supervisor and the Officer in Charge of Interrogations, as well as the JAG. The plan delineated the objective and methods to be used in the interrogation. Upon our request, the MPs brought the detainee in for questioning. The MPs would sign the detainee over to the interrogator. The medical team would give the detainee a physical exam to determine if there were signs of abuse before the interrogation commenced. The interrogation would commence. During the interrogation, the analyst would make notes and together with the interrogator, would compile a report based on the interrogation. This report was sent to the Intelligence Control Element (ICE) and any valuable information was put into an intelligence information report (IIR) and disseminated to other intelligence agencies around the world. The ICE also received requests for intelligence information from other units, which were in turn passed to the interrogation section for inclusion in interrogations.

As we focused on more humane interrogations, we needed some tools to support us in this effort. The members of the Behavioral Scientist Consultation Team (BSCT) had worked with Special Operations at Ft. Bragg and were skilled at offering tools to use in interrogations. The BSCT would view initial interrogations from a viewing room. They identified through observing subtle body responses (i.e., a twitch, crossing or uncrossing a leg, or a sense of general discomfort) a topic or questions for whatever reasons made the detainee uncomfortable. They would help the interrogator incorporate this information into the Interrogation Plan. This was especially helpful for higher profile detainees. The BSCT was also able to suggest better ways of getting information than those seen used by tough guys in the movies, who shouted, cursed, threatened, and/or beat the prisoner to get answers. We had much success using this team and were able to improve the quantity and quality of interrogations.

Additionally, I required the section chiefs, Supervisors, JAG officers, and others in charge, including myself, to observe interrogations, on an impromptu basis any time of the day or night. With these measures, including videotaping the Interrogations, Interrogation Plans being reviewed, and health screenings by the medical team, it would have been close to impossible for any abuse to occur.

The Interrogations were conducted in "CONNEXs" which were large metal containers used by the army for shipping supplies. We had three CONNEXs, and each CONNEX was divided into 4 interrogation rooms and a viewing room. The interrogation rooms were sparse, containing only a folding table and three folding chairs. The detainee sat across from the interrogator, and the translator sat behind the detainee to ensure the focus of the interrogation was between the detainee and interrogator, not the translator. We also had cameras in each of the interrogation rooms, which fed into the viewing room, to record the interrogations.

Some of the interrogators were inexperienced, straight out of the Interrogation Course. Although many of the more seasoned interrogators were good, the new ones, fresh out of school, had some difficulties, but almost across the board, the newly trained female soldiers tended to be better interrogators than the new males. I attributed it to the fact females are often raised to be more intuitive, catching the nuances of a conversation or body language. Much of interrogation is intuitive. We even had one female interrogator, who was proposed to by a detainee. He told her she could be one of his wives, but she would not be allowed to wear make-up all the time, only when she was home alone with him. The unit from Korea had additional challenges: they were used to interrogating North Koreans who were willing participants and came to the Army unit in Korea, hoping to exchange information for a chance at a better life. Interrogating skeptical and sometimes angry Iraqis was not the same thing.

Iraqis have a keen sense of family. Iraqi family loyalty takes precedence over individual achievement. So, it is not a good thing for an Iraqi youngster to go off on his own to make something of himself. His success would not matter if he deserted his family in the process. Iraqis wanted a safe place to live and raise their families, as much as we do here in the States. It was essential for an Iraqi to maintain a sense of honor, dignity and to save face. Many were dissatisfied with the situation in Iraq. Our interrogators needed to keep these things in mind when creating an Interrogation Plan. They needed to find a manner of questioning allowing an Iraqi to admit his guilt or share information while saving face. Once they grasped we were not going to torture them, many became exceedingly cooperative. We had one detainee who was willing to give us information on some key people for a Burger King hamburger.

There were some detainees who unquestionably left an impression on me. The first I'll call Ameriki. His father was Iraqi and his mother American, so because of his dual citizenship status, a Federal Bureau of Investigation (FBI) agent was sent in to interrogate him. I know the FBI has some great investigators and they do an amazing job, but this FBI agent spent about 30 minutes with Ameriki and concluded Ameriki was not going to tell him anything and he was a waste of FBI time. To ensure our measures and restrictions were maintained in the interrogation booth, we always had one of our interrogators, and/or an analyst in the booth with the representative from another government agency or another country during the interrogation. In this case it was an enlisted female, who coincidentally also was working on a master's degree. This soldier was sharp and an astute interrogator. She came to me afterwards and anxiously shared, "Ma'am, I could get Ameriki to talk to me, if I could have a shot at interrogating him." We had nothing to lose, and I trusted this soldier's instincts and gave her the green light. A week later, we had over 100 Intelligence Information Reports (IIRs) with information Ameriki provided. Ameriki was close friends with Saddam; they married each other's sisters or cousins. He gave us information on Saddam's modus operandi (MO) as well as insights to his character and personality. At one point, he offered, "If you let me go, I know Saddam will try to contact me and I can lead you to him." Well, this wasn't going to happen, and after a while, he grew frustrated with us, and the information ceased. In a male dominated society such as Iraq, a female interrogator throws men off. But in Ameriki's case, he seemed to be intrigued by the knowledge and intelligence of his interrogator.

Japan had kamikaze pilots who flew death missions in WWII. The men who hijacked the planes and flew into the Twin Towers in NYC and the Pentagon were on a suicide mission. In Iraq, there were suicide bombers who drove cars filled with explosives and detonated them at an identified target location. Although there are varied reasons why someone would accept these suicide missions, in Iraq, it was a form of Jihad. Jihad has a range of interpretations, from struggling internally to overcome evil tendencies, to a wartime interpretation of fighting against infidels. Terrorists used the word to encourage suicide missions.

Another source of intelligence for the JIDC was a man we referred to as "Burnie." Burnie was a Saudi who was an adventurous young man. He had heard about Jihad: "This is for me. I will live my faith and commit to Jihad." Burnie was committed to his faith. So, he found someone who offered to get him over the border into Iraq. Once in Iraq, he was introduced to someone who could teach him about Jihad. But Burnie soon learned things are not always what they seem. The people Burnie met when he first arrived in Iraq were radical elements who immediately took away his identification/passport and sent him to a training camp. There, he was given drugs and brainwashed; he was taught how to make IEDs, to fire a weapon, and to fight. He and many other young men of similar circumstances were duped. It reminds me of the stories we heard about Charles Manson, back in the 80s. These young men were trained as terrorists and sent on suicide missions, Jihad, in the name of Allah. If they were reluctant or objected, they were told, "You have no identification, no money, and you cannot go home. You might as well die a martyr for your faith and make your life worth something." The day came when Burnie was sent on a suicide mission. He was to drive his car to a designated spot in Baghdad and detonate the bomb. When Burnie was reluctant (he wasn't ready yet), they told him, "Well, park the car and get out. Once you clear the vehicle, we will remotely detonate." Instead, it was detonated the second he tried to exit the vehicle, and he had burns over 70% of his body. He was initially taken to an Iraqi hospital, but they didn't do much for him and he finally was sent to our hospital at Abu Ghraib, which was one of, if not the best in Iraq. The staff cared for his wounds and treated his burns and did skin grafts. We were the first people to sincerely try to help Burnie. After his betrayal, Burnie was disillusioned with the group who recruited him, and wanted to tell his story. He provided valuable information on the training he received as a would-be terrorist, as well as where the training camp was located and how he was misled. He was not alone; we found many of the people killed in suicide missions were not Iraqis at all, but young people from other Middle Eastern countries.

So, what became of Burnie? He provided so much information, we coordinated with the Saudi government to extradite him. He would have to serve some time, but their intent was to make a video to be broadcast on local Saudi televisions, where he could tell his story: what he thought, what he was told and the reality of the terrorist version of Jihad, perhaps preventing other young men from making the same mistake.

In fact, we met with other Middle Eastern governments, when some of their citizens were brought in and interrogated and developed similar programs with them for bringing their young men home and creating more anti-propaganda advertisements.

While at Abu Ghraib, we brought in a training team from Fort Huachuca to conduct a six-week Interrogation School for selected Iraqis—people selected from the military, Department of Interior and Department of Defense. The school focused on interrogation techniques which did not involve maiming, torturing and other more primitive means of interrogation. Many were confused and skeptical of the effectiveness of these "more humane" techniques, but after going through the course, they became believers and saw how it could be much more effective for getting more accurate information. We taught them the Geneva Conventions and required them to sign statements attesting they understood the intent as well as the details. They were also taught the detailed measures we had put in place. We taught them to know whom they were interrogating so they could find other ways to motivate them to talk.

There were 20 people in this course, but only two of them spoke English, so we used one of our interpreters to translate the training. During the course, I got to know some members of the class, especially the ones who spoke English. I had long discussions with them, and I found them to be well educated. I was also surprised to find many of them were extremely conservative. There was one young man, a student in this class, who was a lawyer in the Iraqi Special Forces. He spoke English well, and we had numerous conversations over the duration of the class. He had the same aspirations and desires as most young people in America. He wanted to get married and have a safe place to raise his family. He wanted to enjoy life and live it in comfort. He was smart, good looking and dedicated to his country and making it a better place. When I found out he was single, I said, "You should meet my niece—you would be perfect for each other." Did I foolishly offer to introduce my niece to an Iraqi soldier? HMMMMMMM. Maybe this wasn't my best idea.

At the end of the class, we hosted a class party for the students. Afterwards, we sat around a fire, relaxing and conversing. I decided to tell them a joke. Of course, there was a delay in laughter, because an interpreter had to translate my joke, line by line. Soon, we were matching jokes. One of the Iraqi students would tell a joke, then one of the Americans would. Some of the jokes didn't seem as funny—maybe something was lost in translation. Ironically, many of their jokes were targeted at Saddam, and there was a lot of hooting and laughing when one of those jokes was told. I found humor is universal. At the party, they started singing and dancing, the old ethnic dances done at weddings or other happy occasions. This was weird, until I remembered doing the Chicken Dance at some of my family weddings. Maybe I had no room to talk.

I spoke at their graduation ceremony, attended by many of their supervisors from work. In my address, I had the opportunity to acknowledge them: they were making history. I saw them as the future leaders in Iraq. I admired their patriotism and courage, especially coming to Abu Ghraib, where both our countries have horrible memories. I acknowledged their love of country and their commitment to making Iraq a better place. After the ceremony, the members of the class stated the whole experience gave them a better knowledge of Americans and what we were trying to do in Iraq. Also, the young Iraqi SF man I mentioned earlier introduced me to his boss. I told him my son was in the Special Forces, and I had a great respect for

Special Forces soldiers. Without hesitation, he ripped off his SF arm patch and handed it to me. I was shocked and grateful at the same time. What a generous gesture.

About halfway through my tour, MG Brandenburg, some members of my command and I had an idea to try a different interrogation technique. We transformed one of the CONNEXs into a "comfort suite." We put drywall on the walls and ceilings and painted it. We tiled the floor and put in air conditioning. We put in a Hookah, an Iraqi teapot and tea, a Koran, some prayer rugs, a cushioned chair, and a TV. Additionally, we provided some Iraqi pastries. Of course, we all wanted to move in. We had an Iraqi named Ishmael who was working with us and giving us bits and pieces of information, some extremely relevant. However, we believed he had a critical piece of information he wouldn't share. So, after a couple hours of interrogation, we took him aside. "Ishmael, we've been talking for a while. I am sure you're tired, maybe hungry and could use a break. Why don't you come in here and relax for a while?" We took him into the "comfort suite," where the TV was broadcasting an Iraqi news program. His eyes got as big as saucers as he looked around at the surroundings. He had not had any contact with the outside world, except through visitors, and here was a TV with Iraqi news. "Would you like to hang out here awhile?" And as he emphatically shook his head "Yes." We turned off the TV. "Great. Okay, but first there are a couple more questions we have for you. . ." It worked.

During my time in Iraq, we were heavily into discussions to transition detainee operations to the Iraqis. But the Iraqis worried if we left prematurely, it would be too easy to fall back into old habits and ways of doing things. This was also one of our biggest concerns. Different, more workable attitudes and priorities needed to be internalized, and this takes time. For example, the military leaders seemed to be more concerned with getting all their weapons and tanks than taking care of their soldiers and getting them paid. Many soldiers left the military because they couldn't live on $5 a month. This mindset needed to change. They needed to believe self-determination and self-government is possible, and they could be part of this endeavor or they would be sidelined and marginalized. When we presented this to the detainees, many of them were willing to work with us. We appealed to their sense of patriotism and family values and motivated them to help make a better Iraq for their children. This was what we wanted, as well.

Eric Maddox, known as the person responsible for collecting evidence to locate Saddam Hussein, was quoted as saying, "The (interrogation) techniques I was trained on didn't work, and it wasn't because I was a bad interrogator, they just didn't work in this new type of warfare. The techniques the Army emphasized were confrontational, threatening and intimidating, and they caused hopelessness rather than building trust." Under MG Brandenburg's leadership, we at the Joint Interrogation and Debriefing Center put measures in place to protect the humanity of each Iraqi we interrogated. We were sensitive to the values of the Iraqi people. We were creative and initiated new means of interrogation exceeding our expectations for effectiveness. We proved we could get more intelligence through compassion and respect than we could through previously used brutal methods. The military men and women who worked for me could leave this tour proud of what they accomplished. Their success restored their pride in being an interrogator. This was another aspect of the human dimension of men in battle.

22

Command: Challenges and Rewards

A Commander hears everything. Before the new unit arrived, I heard the contractors stationed at Abu Ghraib, who were providing some of the building structures and drinking water, were making bets on who could be the first to get one of the new females into bed. When the unit arrived, I called all the females in for a meeting. I told them of the rumors and I led a discussion on professionalism, loyalty (to partners and personal values), propriety in the workplace, integrity, reputations, appearances, and consequences. We also discussed sexual harassment, and I told them if any of the men made comments, gestures or actions offending them or made them uncomfortable to let me know immediately. During the conversation, one of the girls admitted being approached by a contractor. "He was so nice." She kept saying. "We connected." The conversation took off. Other women started telling their stories. I don't know how much this "intervention" helped the women in my command but hopefully the awareness prevented at least some of the female soldiers from doing something they regretted or getting into an uncomfortable position. I did send one soldier home who got pregnant while assigned there. The female soldier related her relationship was consensual; she was not sent home for punishment, but for mission requirements. We did this to keep her and her baby safe, as well as make sure everyone in the unit could perform his/her mission.

Commanding the JIDC was a tough assignment for me. It wasn't the conditions, which became my new normal. It wasn't the separation from home, because I talked to the kids on a weekly basis and exchanged emails and letters with friends and family, who were supportive and were praying for me. It was the responsibility of command, not only for the mission but also for the personnel. This is why I talked to the new females. This is also why the tension between the augmentees and the new unit concerned me. Before morale dropped too low, some team building needed to be done. I told everyone in the unit who was not on duty on one Sunday afternoon to assemble outside the briefing area in PT clothes. Everyone. No exceptions. There were all kinds of rumors going around: "We are going to fill sandbags." "We are pulling extra duty." When they arrived, I selected four section leaders and told them they had to pick unit members until everyone was on a team. Each team had to be composed of Officers, Enlisted, Translators, Individual Augmentees, and DoD Civilians from all elements of the JIDC. I had devised routes with ten checkpoints. For example, one checkpoint required the team to get some cold drinks and take it to the Marines protecting the outer perimeter; another checkpoint required each member of the team to shoot a basket at the gym; another checkpoint required answering a question about the Geneva Conventions; etc. Each team took a different route, but they all had to cover the same ten checkpoints. The first team to complete the route won a day off (coordinated with their immediate supervisor). When everyone returned, I had coordinated with the dining facility for a cookout. Mess hall personnel came to the JIDC area and barbequed steaks, with all the trimmings. Everyone enjoyed dinner together as they discussed the event. Maybe tensions returned the next day, but for a short time on this one day, everyone enjoyed themselves and got along with people they hadn't bothered with before.

On Mother's Day, at our weekly staff meeting, the unit presented me with a card—not any store-bought card—a 3-foot by 4-foot card saying, "Happy Mother's Day, Colonel Rogers, from all your boys and girls at Abu Ghraib." I was moved and faced with the realization sometimes I was a mother as well as a commander, to these young soldiers, airmen, sailors, and Marines comprising my unit. I remember one Major, who, at a Staff meeting, meant to say, "Yes, ma'am" and inadvertently responded to my question with "Yes, Mom."

Around this time, I took leave and went home for my son's graduation from high school and my niece's wedding. Frank obtained his high school diploma through online courses from James Madison University. I was so proud of his diligence and persistence. Through email, we worked together to put together invitations and plan a celebration back in Buffalo for all our relatives. My niece's wedding was also in Buffalo at the same time. I was so happy to honor and be there to share Frank's success. It was great to see my children, as well as my extended family. However, part of me was still in Iraq, concerned about the people, the unit, the mission. It was more difficult going back than it was going the first time, as now I knew what to expect and I was aware of what I was going back to. But there was also a familiarity providing a comfort level. It was a weird combination.

I was gone for one week. When I returned, I heard my XO (LTC Brownnose) had put out the order that end of tour awards would be less for those who had not been there for a full year. The Individual Augmentees were assigned from 6 to 9 months, and some were finishing their tour; so, it seemed this order was directed towards them. Considering these people were working 14 to 18-hour days prior to the new unit arriving, and considering their productivity, this was grossly unfair. I called my XO in and he denied it. So, I immediately put out a directive stating awards would be based on merit, not longevity. Some military members accomplish more in a week than others accomplish in a year, and they would be awarded accordingly. This was one of many confrontations I had with my XO, and he never owned his comments and actions. Moreover, during the week I went home for the graduation and wedding, I heard he often held back pieces of intelligence information until the following day, instead of sending Intelligence Information reports in as they were produced, in case he did not have anything to report the next day. When I questioned him about these allegations, he denied them, and all I had was hearsay. I wanted to believe him. I wanted him to be a person of integrity and honor. So, I gave him the benefit of doubt and resolved to watch him closely.

We had monthly ceremonies within the unit, where we acknowledged re-enlistments, awards, and promotions. Additionally, I started asking the Section Chiefs for the names of people who had worked particularly hard or who accomplished something particularly significant during the month, and we printed a certificate for them and took the time to acknowledge them at our monthly ceremony. I also coordinated with the D-FAC (dining facility) to bake us a cake and we added monthly birthdays to the monthly agenda. The JIDC members started looking forward to these monthly ceremonies. I hoped this would help take the edge off long days in this war-torn country, far from home. This provided many opportunities for each of us to relax and enjoy ourselves and each other.

We learned at the War College leadership has many dimensions and considerations. My boss in Iraq, MG Brandenburg was the best officer I worked for in all my time in the Army. He was combat arms, an Armor Officer, but he had great military intelligence instincts. He proves what I was told by the hardcore troops (SF, Rangers, First Cavalry and XVIII Airborne), "the best MI officers are the ones with a combat arms background, because they have a full scope of battlefield operations. Too many MI officers have tunnel vision." MG

Brandenburg demonstrated all the qualities of a good leader I studied at the AWC. He had a great strategic vision for Detainee Operations at Abu Ghraib, and he interfaced with all of us (the hospital, the Post and the JIDC) to optimize our effectiveness. He assumed leadership, not control. He welcomed feedback. He was not driven by personal power or recognition, but by a sense of a higher purpose. Plus, he supported me as a Commander, mentored me and allowed me to do my job with minimal oversight. I was fortunate to have him as my supervisor for this command.

My unit outdid themselves for my farewell. The week prior to departure, my unit surprised me by asking me to come by the dayroom in the makeshift barracks they lived in. I came in, and they placed me in a chair before a large movie screen and they proceeded to present a slideshow of pictures taken during my time at Abu Ghraib. They concluded with a video of each of them saying good-bye to me and commenting on our time together. They also presented some small, but significant gifts from the sections. One was a plaque a major had carved himself. On the plaque was embedded a gear from one of the rockets found outside the perimeter, from the attack on Abu Ghraib in April. The translators gave me an Iraqi tea set. The medical unit gave me a box containing various remembrances from Abu Ghraib (a piece of fabric from the jumpsuits worn by the detainees; a piece of barbed wire from our perimeter; a pouch of sand from the compound). Plus, they gave me CDs of the pictures and videos I had watched. I was so moved and touched by the effort and time they put into the farewell. Even more rewarding are the grateful comments I receive to this day whenever I encounter one of the members of my unit. At the end of my tour, when I took stock of what we accomplished as a unit, all the statistics measuring the quantity and quality of the intelligence gleaned through interrogations, and the sense of humanity we brought to the treatment of the detainees, I am filled with pride for all the members of the JIDC and what they accomplished. I hope they all left with the same sense of pride in themselves I have in them. They worked hard, in an unpleasant environment, confined to a compound, with little to distract them from the situation at hand. Leadership is not about the leader; it is about the subordinates and the success of their efforts. I came to Iraq for the MI military members, to restore their sense of pride in themselves and their mission. I scheduled a monthly meeting to acknowledge individuals and their accomplishments. I listened to their concerns and addressed them. I endeavored to create cohesiveness and acceptance through a team building exercise. I made mistakes; there were times I could have been stronger. Did I cut my XO too much slack? When I consider the rating MG Brandenburg gave me, I am assured. I am humbled by the words of praise which came from a man I admired so much. In my end-of-tour award, I was proud of his acknowledgement of the achievements the JIDC attained during my time there, but I was most touched by his statement, "Despite a litany of challenges and the relentless intelligence demands required while in theater, COL Rogers' leadership and reliable mentorship served as a reminder to all of what is good and decent in our nation and validated to those who serve that our values remain alive and well in the best of our Soldiers, Sailors, Airmen, Marines and civilians operating in the JIDIC." This was exactly what I hoped to achieve.

23

Leaving: You CAN Go Home Again

Soon, it came time to leave Iraq. My tour was over. A bittersweetness swept over me. What I was doing in Iraq was important, and there still was so much more to do. We hadn't found PFC Maupin. We didn't find the weapons of mass destruction (WMD). The Iraqi government was not yet stable. They weren't prepared yet to take over the Interrogation mission, which was our goal. Saddam was in custody but had not yet been to trial. And I was leaving. My replacement arrived and a Change of Command scheduled.

As my departure became imminent, I started saying goodbye and thank you to the people around the post. When I took my clothes to the laundry, I told them I was leaving and going home. The Iraqi woman who worked there followed me out and held my hands as she started to cry, "Thank you for everything you did here. I admire you so much. Come back in the evening to get your clothes—I have something for you." I had never had any kind of in-depth conversation with this woman; she genuinely caught me off guard. When I returned in the evening, she had my laundry and a couple Iraqi scarves. Her generosity and thoughtfulness truly touched me. But mostly, I was astounded by her impressions of me. I can't remember doing anything that would have moved her one way or another. We never know how we touch people.

When I was about to take my last trip to Camp Victory for the weekly staff meeting, I told Top I wanted to man the gun, the .50 caliber machine gun in the high mobility multipurpose wheeled vehicle (HMMWV). He didn't know what to make of me, but I spent an afternoon familiarizing myself with the weapon, so the people I was traveling with could trust me. I did need a stool, because standing I couldn't see above the turret to aim the weapon. So, on the convoy ride to Camp Victory and back, I was the gunner. It was a rush, but the enormity of the position was not lost on me. I would be the first one to shoot if we were attacked. As I looked through the scope, I had to ask myself if I was ready to shoot someone. It's what I was trained to do, and hopefully the training would kick in, but I am not sure anyone honestly knows for sure how they would react until faced with the choice. I should have taken pictures, but I didn't. And I didn't make a big deal about it. But when I returned to Abu Ghraib, some of the other senior NCO's (from the MPs and Hospital) approached me with praise: "Way to go, ma'am. We saw you manning the gunner. Wait till I tell COL So and So what you did and ask why he never did." I won a few brownie points that day.

In 2005, when I went to Iraq, there was credible evidence we were ridding Iraq of a sadistic dictator. Saddam Hussein's cruelty to his own people is well documented. He was devoid of conscience, and his ruthlessness extended to his own family. Al Jazeera reported in 2004 two of his daughters defected to Jordan in 1995 with their husbands, Kamil and Hussain Kamil. Saddam reportedly pardoned them, and they returned to Baghdad. They were killed upon their arrival. Additionally, Saddam believed in the superiority of the Arab people and culture, much like Hitler in reference to the Germans. Americans erroneously ignored what Hitler was doing to the Jewish people in Germany; we believed this was a second opportunity to rid a country of its ruthless and sadistic dictator. This is what I knew about Saddam going into Iraq.

Also, there was evidence of WMD. The military needed to intervene to protect the US. Although there was evidence surfacing that United Nations (UN) inspectors did not find WMD, there was also credible evidence to the contrary. A few years earlier, Saddam had used extreme measures to keep inspectors out of Iraq. David Kay, an inspector dispatched by the International Atomic Energy Agency (IAEA) reported,

> *Inspectors were awakened with telephoned threats; obscene and threatening notes were slipped under hotel doors; hotel rooms were ransacked; verbal abuse on the street and at inspection sites became common; on several occasions inspectors were physically attacked by outraged Iraqi 'civilians'; UN vehicles were bombed, and tires slashed; and shots were fired over the heads of inspectors as a team photographed Iraq's secret uranium enrichment equipment.*

In the face of Saddam's efforts to prevent inspectors from looking into WMD in Iraq, it was plausible to accept the possibility WMD existed in Iraq.

Was the US effective in Iraq? Based on our beliefs at the time, initially, yes. It did not take long for the coalition forces to overthrow Saddam's regime. However, we created a tactical blunder. We did not have a plan in place for when the war was over. Interesting to note is the president sent us there. Congress, which is key in the system of checks and balances to ensure the rationale for going to war and the policy goals sought by this decision are clearly defined, has not exercised this Constitutional duty since WWII. The US spent months making a post-war plan after the Allies won WWII; however, there was no post-war plan in place after victory in Iraq. We did not have enough forces for the peacekeeping mission following the end of the fighting. Consequently, insurgents from

the Saddam era as well as common criminals looted businesses, cultural centers, and government office buildings, stealing
or destroying great Iraqi artwork. The Iraqis were glad we
put an end to Saddam's cruelty, and now they looked to us to
establish some order, and we stood by and did nothing. We
had no orders to restrain criminals and insurgents. We did a
disservice to the Iraqis by not immediately following through
on our success by putting a peacekeeping force in place.

We fought to bring safety back to the citizens of Iraq. And
after US Forces captured Saddam, he was turned over to the
Iraqis for trial. He was found guilty of crimes against human-
ity and executed by his own people on December 30, 2006.
It was essential for Saddam to be taken to trial, allowing the
Iraqi people to close the page on this part of their history.

Why did I go to Iraq? Looking at Iraq now, more than
15 years later, I am extremely conflicted. So many questions
arise as to what the US was doing in Iraq. Yes, Saddam was a
ruthless dictator, but so were Muammar Gaddafi or Kim Jong
or Idi Amin, but we did not invade Libya or North Korea or
Rwanda. And as for WMD, if Iraq had them, why is there no
evidence of their use in the last 15 years? Was the real motive
oil, as is now commonly believed? Were we all duped to believe something else? Did I have my head in the sand? Should
I have known better? I examined again the reasons I came to
Iraq: to restore a sense of integrity to interrogators and Military Intelligence. The Intel we obtained was not through the
use of force, through deprivation of food or sleep, or through
torture or humiliation. It was by showing the detainees something they never saw under the Saddam regime: respect for
human dignity. This is what America was known for, and
even despite the scandals we have had, the world still expects
this is the basic premise we operate under. And our young
interrogators were able to show this respect to the detainees,
because they were raised in a country that fosters these ideals.
American people have made mistakes, but American values

are still intact. I want to believe this. I must believe this, or the basic foundation of my beliefs and service to my country becomes suspect. I recognize sometimes evidence of this may be challenged, but when I look around, I am constantly seeing evidence—in the men and women who serve in the military, in the people who fight for equality and freedom, and in those who give their time tirelessly to helping those less fortunate. This is the America I serve, and I believe in.

Prior to coming to Iraq, I discussed ideologies, and commented on the stories in the paper. However, living here it became all too real. The experience of being in a country like Iraq, where people lived in fear of senseless murder and brutality as the norm for life, was sadly an eye opener. I took so much for granted. Having served here, I will never be able to look at the value of freedom complacently again.

When I left Iraq, I went via the Baghdad military airport, to Kuwait, and on to the States. The military airport there was different from what you might be used to. My four duffle bags of military gear and one suitcase sat on a tarmac waiting to be bundled for the plane. There was no porter to carry my bags, nor was there a luggage cart to rent. The passenger terminal was the tent to the far right. I went to a desk, where my paperwork was verified. Otherwise, I could not leave the country. I checked a whiteboard, where the next flights were listed. I watched as they canceled one, delayed another. I was placed on a space available list and waited for my flight.

Military members waited in the passenger tent. There were some cots, some folding chairs, and it was hot and crowded. The ever-present porta-potty was outside, as was a PX if there were last minute items you needed to purchase.

I was in the next tent. Seems I ranked a seat in the VIP tent. There we had a couple couches and a computer. So, with time on my hands, which I did not have for a while, I started writing some notes about my experience. I wish I had kept a journal. I started, but usually I was so tired when I finally got to my hooch at night, I immediately crashed. But I wish I had recorded everything, because as I was leaving, the last 8 months were slipping away. Already, it was hazy. Was I actually in a warzone?

Since I was the senior person in the group, I was the "movement commander." This would have been an easy task if our flight had gone as scheduled. However, there was delay after delay and after the second day went by, folks were getting extremely antsy and irritable. Between trying to get accurate information from the flight staff and calming my fellow travelers, my time was pretty busy. Finally, the day came, and we boarded the aircraft and took off. We were on our way home. We were placed on a contracted commercial airline, so we had a civilian pilot and flight attendants. Coming home, as we crossed into Maine, the pilot announced, "We have entered US airspace." Everyone started hooting and hollering and crying. I choked remembering this. It is so difficult to explain to someone who never experienced deployment to a war zone, but the whole experience of being in Iraq made all of us intensely present to the freedoms we enjoy in the US. The pilots told us they were buying all of us a drink to celebrate.

We had to stop in Bangor to refuel and we had to deplane. The time was about 4 a.m. As we got off the plane, local people had gathered and were on either side of the runway as we walked in, and they all were shaking our hands and thanking us for our service. I was so emotional I couldn't speak. I was home. These were my people. They were acknowledging my service and ME. This still moves me in ways touching the depth of my soul. They had fresh sandwiches, baked goods, drinks, and cell phones for each of us to use and call loved ones waiting to hear from us. They were composed of retired military, as well as families and friends who volunteered to come to the airport any time a flight was due in from Iraq. I will always remember these people for making our homecoming so meaningful.

Finally, it was on to Fort Dix for physicals and out-processing, and arrangements for our final flight home. I arrived at Reagan International, where some friends and my sons greeted me with balloons and smiles and hugs. It was so good to be home and hold my children. More tears. I walked through the airport and strangers thanked me for my service. To this day, I am still so moved when I hear the words, "Thank you for your service." These words mean so much to all of us who have served and believe service to our country is an honorable thing. It still tugs at my heart every time I hear them. Thanks to all of you for your acknowledgements.

24

Dad: Full Circle

When I returned to the G-2 and home, everything was running smoothly. Want to know how much your absence will impact your organization? Put your hand in a pail of water and remove it. The hole left is the impact your absence will make. When I returned, my old division was operating smoothly. But some personnel had left, so I was transferred to the technical side of Intelligence Operations—Surveillance Division—same directorate, different division. The folks in this division oversee Signals Intelligence (SIGINT), Imagery Intelligence (IMINT), Measurement and Signals Intelligence (MASINT), Weather, Geospatial Information Services, Geo-Intelligence, and Space activities, ensuring national systems and architectures met and addressed Army equities. I was responsible for coordinating and promulgating policies and program requirements at the Army, National, and Joint levels. Since none of this was my intelligence area of expertise, I depended immensely on the folks who worked for me to inform me and brief me on these areas. They were all geeks, great at their jobs, and had been doing this for most of their careers.

There were some impacts from my time in Iraq. I could not sleep at night, and I could not stay awake during the day. This lasted for almost two months. I dozed off while one of my new teams was briefing me. I dozed off at video conferences with other units. I tried everything—pumping myself full of caffeine, chewing gum, constantly drinking water, tea, and caffeinated drinks, eating, pinching myself—nothing worked. It was embarrassing, and I didn't know what to do. Finally, I decided to see a doctor. Doc said a high percentage of people returning from Iraq had sleep issues. He gave me some pills to help me sleep, and I guess getting a better sleep at night helped me stay awake during the day.

I was also surprised the G-2 leadership seemed to lack interest in hearing about my experiences in Iraq. I did have limited talks with the G-2, but they barely scratched the surface. However, when I returned from Iraq, GEN Cody, formerly the G-3 who headed the Saturday video-conferences with the leaders down-range, was now serving as Vice Chief of Staff of the Army, the second highest ranking officer on active duty in the army. While I had never worked for GEN Cody, he sent me a letter thanking me for my service and asking me to please stay in the Army, because the Army needed the expertise of officers who had served in the Middle East. I was moved that even though I never worked for him and he only knew me from various meetings I attended, he made the effort to send a letter to me. Imagine me, a Colonel getting a letter from a 4-Star General. What a testament to the quality of officer he was.

My younger boys were both getting on with their lives. Frank had his high school diploma and had started taking courses towards an associate degree at Northern Virginia College. Joe was in his second year at Northwestern and was already aiming for the stars. He was working toward (and earned) a triple major—Industrial Engineering, Political Science, and Economics. He requested to be sent to Egypt for a semester. He was caddying and getting career advice from the Presidents and CEOs of companies who were members of Old Elm, where he still caddied during the summers. He has since attained all the goals he set for himself, and reconnected and married Lindsey, a girl he went to highschool with. All my children made great choices for partners!

After my return, many civic and religious organizations were interested in my story, and I provided many presentations talking about my time in Iraq. The response, following my presentation, was always the same, "Why didn't we know this?" "This is not what I was reading in the papers." I spoke to a group outside of Boston, and they put it on their local cable TV station, as well as paying for my travel to Boston. I spoke on leadership to a group of officers at the Director of National Intelligence Office and used my experience working under MG Brandenburg in Iraq to highlight my philosophy of leadership and experiences in Iraq. I loved sharing my stories, and this is one of the reasons I am writing this book.

It was less than a year after I returned from Iraq when I received notice from Army Personnel that my Mandatory Removal Date (MRD) was imminent. I had to retire. I went through the drill of requesting an extension, requesting to stay beyond my MRD, including GEN Cody's letter, but my request was denied. This time the Army was making me do something I didn't want to do. This time my letter did not change their mind. I had to retire. I guess it was time. I had always planned to stay in until it wasn't fun anymore, but it was time to leave, and I was still having fun.

Ceremonies are part of military tradition and retirement farewells are even more so. My unit outdid themselves for mine, and there was a special event I want to note. My immediate supervisor at the time was a huge Red Sox Fan. So, he planned an evening for the whole Directorate to go to Camden Yards in Baltimore to watch the Red Sox play the Orioles. He insisted I go, and as busy as I was with the entire administrative retirement minutia, I finally relented. We were all enjoying the game, when between innings, the marquee lights: "Thanks to COL Carol Rogers for her 32 years of service in the US Army." I was shocked and turned to ask him if he did this, and someone shot a picture. They later gave me the picture. There I am smiling and in the background behind me clear as day is the marquee. What a marvelous gift and one I will always treasure and remember at every ballgame I ever attend.

Hearing everything I have shared about my army career, it should not be surprising I planned an extensive ending. Because so many friends and relatives would be coming in from out of town, and would need a place to stay, and would be looking to me for things to do, I decided I would plan events for folks to attend. If they wanted to participate, great. If they had their own plans, they could go off on their own. I reserved a block of rooms at a convenient hotel and sent out invitations with a four-day itinerary. On Thursday afternoon, at Ft. Myer, there was a group retirement recognizing all local military officers and enlisted who were retiring. Part of the ceremony included the Drum and Bugle Corps demonstration, as well as a presentation by the Old Guard. I loved being included in such a great display of Army discipline. It reminded me of the parades I was in as a young officer and how much I loved the precision of marching. All the folks who came in on Thursday to attend this were impressed and glad they attended. My actual retirement ceremony was on Friday. I had decided I wanted to have my ceremony in the chapel. My faith sustained me throughout all the difficult times of my career, and it seemed fitting for me to end my career in a chapel. So, I had an award ceremony in the General's Conference Room, followed by a Prayer Service in the Memorial Chapel. The day concluded with a party I hosted in the Community Room of my condo. I had almost two hundred guests that day, and there was a steady stream of people stopping in, from 4:00 until midnight when the last person left. The next day, I planned a bike ride around the national monuments for everyone who wanted to bike and a trolley tour of DC for all others. I wanted my family and friends to get a taste of the city where I lived and worked in for so many years, its history and its grandeur. Afterwards, I planned a group dinner for everyone, and for anyone who was still standing, I planned a Ghost Tour of old town Alexandria later in the evening. Sunday, we went to the National Shrine of the Immaculate Conception for Mass, followed by a brunch at the Fort Belvoir Officers Club. It seems excessive, and my friend Colonel Ted Drier teased me about being the only person who needed four days to retire. However, I truly needed the time to accept the fact my Army days were over. This was not only a way of life for 32 years; it was my life. Mentally, I knew when I took the uniform off, no one would surely care what I used to do. Realizing this made it especially difficult.

The prayer service was the meat of my ceremony. Prayer was where I went when I was overwhelmed or lost or needed answers. This is where I found peace and strength, a sense of direction, sometimes a little wisdom or discernment. So, it was fitting I acknowledge the role of faith and prayer in my military service and selected the chapel for my final hoorah. I chose some Bible readings which some of the people I worked with read. Another man who worked for me offered to sing. He had to sing a cappella, as there was no music available in the chapel. I had never heard him sing prior to the ceremony, but I could not have hired a professional who had a more beautiful voice. Attached is the agenda for the Retirement Prayer Service, and you can see the beautiful songs he sang, as well as my acknowledgements of the people who impacted my life during my military career.

My award ceremony was the official ending of my career. I had so many people in attendance they did not all fit in the General's Conference Room, so they brought in a camera and fed the video into a second conference room.

I received various presentations and gifts from members of the G-2 Team, my retirement letter, and as the General called

"ATTENTION TO ORDERS" to present my military end-of-career award and everyone came to attention, unbeknownst to me, my mother is raising her hand, saying, "Excuse me, Excuse me. . ." So, the General stopped and noted that someone wanted to say something. Mom tells some story she remembered from my military career. I was so mortified, aware my mom was interrupting a time-honored military tradition. I don't even remember the story. But the General was cool, let her have her say, and continued with my award presentation.

I was so moved when I looked out at the audience to see my co-workers, past and present, and friends as well as military members I had served with at Ft Huachuca, Ft. Sheridan, the Pentagon, and Iraq, who traveled hundreds of miles to be there with me for my retirement. Additionally, there were so many family members who traveled in to witness the last of my military ceremonies, most notably my parents and my sons who were always there for me. They are all part of my story and I owe a debt of gratitude to each of them.

After giving me my award, the general concluded with a story. Sometime prior to my ceremony, he inquired if anyone in my family was a military member. I told him about my father, how he had won a Purple Heart and Silver Star in WWII. Well, unbeknownst to me, he had someone on his staff research my dad's unit and he proceeded at my ceremony to acknowledge my dad and tell the story of the campaign his unit was involved in. I couldn't have been prouder of my dad and my military heritage.

So now I have come full circle: From the young girl who decided to join the Army because of her father's military service, to this aging soldier who, with her father, was honored at a retirement ceremony, some 32 years later. My father was the real soldier. He put his life on the line; he was the hero. I will always pale in comparison, but I will always be grateful for these 32 years, the places I have been, the experiences and opportunities I have had, and especially the people I have worked with and met throughout my career. There was never one moment when I did not believe I was exactly where God meant for me to be and doing what He meant for me to do.

It has been years since I took my uniform off, and I continue to persist. My children are grown and no longer need my daily care. However, I am still persevering in deepening those relationships. I am still a mom; I won't take that uniform off.

I didn't follow the path "society" says is the way to success. I made decisions making "society" raise its arms in exasperation. But I plowed through the only way I knew how: by working hard, adapting to whatever twists and turns life presented, accepting the consequences of my actions, and believing. My faith sustained me when there was nothing else.

Since my retirement, I pass hundreds of people as I walk through town in my civilian clothes. No one salutes; passer-byers don't acknowledge my service. However, my uniform hangs in my closet, with all my medals and awards, as an occasional reminder of this amazing part of my life. My uniform symbolizes my accomplishments. What I carry away inside of me after those 32 years of service is persistence, adaptability, determination, acceptance, and faith—traits all learned as a child, but honed as a soldier, making possible all those accomplishments. These are the same tools I will use going forward, because I still have things to do, I am still growing and learning. This is not the end of my story; it is simply the last chapter I wrote. There will always be another chapter.

Epilogue

It has been fifteen years since I retired and began writing this book. My parents have both since died and they were interred at Arlington Cemetery, where my father was recognized and honored "by a grateful nation" for his service to our country.

My relationships with my daughters remain strained, but I have spoken to Kelly and have seen Amy, her husband, and my granddaughters at Joe and Frank's weddings. Joe and Frank now have their own families, and have given me two more granddaughters, Sadie (two years old) and Evelyn (four months old). My children are all productive members of society who have done extremely well in their chosen professions. They each chose the perfect spouse for themselves and have good, solid marriages (which I consider an amazing feat, given my track record). I believe in them and will continue to work on good relationships with all of them.

Nine years ago I met and a year later married Grady, my gift from God. I am blessed to be married to a man who makes me a better person; who works with me each day to make our marriage stronger and better. He believes in me and makes me believe in myself. We continue to grow as individuals and work on the intricacies of relationships with the people we love. We try to stay physically fit so we can enjoy the years to come.

Retirement Prayer Service

Please Rise for the Entrance of the Chaplain
*Song: Morning Has Broken
Welcome by the Chaplain
First Reading: Ecclesiastes 3:13 (COL Artero)
*Song: Just a Closer Walk with Thee
Second Reading: 1 Corinthians 12:12-30 (COL St Cyr)
*Song: We are Many Parts
Gospel Reading: Luke 17:12-19 (Chaplain Bruno)
Bible Reflections: Chaplain Bruno
Prayers of Petition: Mr. Toomey
*Song: Let There be Peace on Earth
Prayers of Thanksgiving: COL Carol Rogers
*Song: God Bless America
*Songs sung by Mr. Mark Miller

The Prayers of Thanksgiving include everything I wanted to say about my military career:

I thank God for all the blessings in my life, especially those received during my time in the Army.

I am thankful for His guidance leading me into the Army 32 years ago.

I am thankful for the opportunities to grow through wonderful assignments and challenging experiences.

I am thankful for the exciting places I have lived.

I am thankful I was led to a profession where members can be proud of our faith in God.

I am thankful to be among people who strive to attain high ideals, and never lower the bar, even when faced with failure.

But mostly, I am thankful for the people that I have been blessed to work with and who have touched my life along the way.

I am thankful for my friends many of whom are here today, who knew me before I went on Active Duty and who have allowed me to share my stories and experiences,

I am thankful for the people I met in joint assignments, who have enriched my life, and brought the perspective of our sister services to me.

I am thankful for the wonderful friends I made at the Army War College, and their spouses, who also became part of my life.

I am thankful for the countless friends I have made in the military, especially all those who I have served with over the years—you know who you are and you will always be in my prayers.

I am thankful for my nieces and nephews, who share their lives with me and have helped keep me young.

I am thankful for my brothers, who have kept me humble over the years, by never letting me forget where I came from and who have always supported me.

I am thankful for the cousins, in-laws, and other family members who have traveled to share this event with me.

I am thankful for my kids' friends, who have been their sounding boards and confidants as they sorted through thoughts and issues connected with their life as a "military brat," or when they needed to complain about me.

I am thankful for the opportunity to deploy and do what we are trained to do—to preserve peace, and I am thankful for the wonderful people who shared this experience with me.

I am thankful for the leadership in the G-2, from LTG Kimmons to the Directors and Division Chiefs—I have never worked with such a professional, dedicated group of people, who couple those great qualities with a wonderful sense of humanity and who have befriended me, and made this an enjoyable place to work.

I am thankful for my Buffalo Buds—who remind me that home is never far away.

And I am especially thankful for all the professionals who "worked for me"—which means they did all the work and I took all the credit—great team leaders and all those on their teams. Thank you all so much for your hard work, long hours, and support.

I am thankful for the remaining G-2 family—all of you who have smiled at me and brightened my day, or answered my request for information, or helped me work on a tasker—thank you for all you do, every day.

I am thankful for the Chaplains, who never let our kids go in harm's way alone, and especially for Chaplain Bruno, for agreeing to lead this prayer service for me.

And I am thankful for my family, including my in-laws who have continued to give me love and support.

I am thankful for my parents who were there for me every step of the way—babysitting kids when I went to Basic Training, attending my commissioning and most of my promotions and my graduation from army schools, and now the finale. Thank you. Dad, it was reading about your wartime experience that filled me with a love of country, honor, and dedication to duty posturing me for success in the military. Thank you for creating this environment for me to grow in. And thank you to Mom, who taught me how to nurture and believe in people, supporting them and caring about them. This combination allowed me to succeed by being who I am.

And finally, I am thankful for my kids. In many ways, our careers are hardest on them—they didn't sign up for this, they simply got dragged along. Thank you, Lord, for helping them adjust to each move, for guiding them to new friends each time we moved and for giving them continued opportunities to grow.

For Bobby, who waited at home while I went off to Basic Training, who pinned my butter bar on me when I was commissioned, who, through his service, taught me about soldiering and who is still sharing my accomplishments (now with his wife, Eva) by being here today—thank you, Bobby.

I am thankful for Joe, who consistently amazes me and makes me proud, and who will make the world a better place, not only by what he will do, but also simply by being in it.

And I am thankful for Frank, who will be the last to leave home when he goes to VA Tech in the fall, who has been my roommate for the last 2 years, whose loving ways and affection have given me so much comfort over the years.

I love you guys and I am so proud and thankful for you!

I have so many blessings, and God sent me His blessings through each of you. Thank you all.

This pretty much sums us the gratitude I have for my 32 years of service—20 on active duty and 12 in the Reserves. It was a great ride.

Acronyms

AFB – Air Force Base

AG – Adjutant General

AGOBC – Adjutant General Officer Basic Course

APFT – Army Physical Fitness Test

ARISC – Army Reserve Intelligence Support Center

ARRTC – Army Reserve Readiness Training Center

AT – Annual Training

ATC – Air Traffic Control

BSCT – Behavioral Scientist Consultation Team

CAR – Chief, Army Reserve

CASP – Civilian Acquired Skills Program

CAT – Crisis Action Team

CO – Commanding Officer

CSM – Command Sergeant Major

D-FAC – Dining Facility

DOB – Date of Birth

DOD – Department of Defense

FBI – Federal Bureau of Investigation

GO – General Officer

GWOT – Global War on Terrorism

HMMWV – High Mobility Multipurpose Wheeled Vehicle

ICE – Intelligence Control Element

IED – Improvised Explosive Device

IIR – Intelligence Information Report

IMA – Individual Mobilization Augmentation

ITAC – Intelligence Threat Analysis Center

ITC – Instructor Training Course

JIDC – Joint Interrogation and Debriefing Center

JRIC – Joint Reserve Intelligence Center

MC – Marine Corps

MI – Military Intelligence

MIOAC – Military Intelligence Officer Advanced Course

MIRC – Military Intelligence Reserve Command

MO – Modus Operandi

MOS – Military Occupational Specialty

MP – Military Police

MRD – Mandatory Removal Date

NATO – North Atlantic Treaty Organization

OBC – Officer Basic Course

OCS – Officer Candidate School

OER – Officer Evaluation Report

OIF – Operation Iraqi Freedom

PLF – Parachute Landing Fall

PT – Physical Training

PTSD – Post Traumatic Stress Disorder

RAF – Red Army Faction

RIID – Reserve Intelligence Integration Division

ROTC – Reserve Officer Training Corps

SA – Special Agent

SACEUR – Supreme Allied Commander, Europe

SES – Senior Executive Service

SHAPE – Supreme Headquarters Allied Powers, Europe

SF – Special Forces

TAC - Tactical

TF – Task Force

USA – United States Army

USARCPAC – United States Army Reserve Personnel Administration Command Center

USDI – Under Secretary of Defense for Intelligence

USMILPERCEN – United States Military Personnel Center

VBIED – Vehicle Borne Improvised Explosive Device

WAC – Women's Army Corps

WMD – Weapons of Mass Destruction

WWII – World War II

XO – Executive Officer

Army Ranks

Enlisted:

- Private (PVT)-E-1
- Private Second Class (PV2)-E-2
- Private First Class (PFC)-E-3
- Specialist (SPC)/Corporal (CPL)-E-4
- Sergeant (SGT)-E-5
- Staff Sergeant (SSG)-E-6
- Sergeant First Class (SFC)-E-7
- Master Sergeant (MSG)/First Sergeant-E-8
- Sergeant Major (SGM)/Command Sergeant Major (CSM)-E-9

Warrant Officer:

- Warrant Officer 1 (WO1)-W-1
- Chief Warrant Officer 2 (CW2)-W-2
- Chief Warrant Officer 3 (CW3)-W-3
- Chief Warrant Officer 4 (CW4)-W-4
- Chief Warrant Officer 5 (CW5)-W-5

Officer:

- Second Lieutenant (2LT)-O-1
- First Lieutenant (1LT)-O-2
- Captain (CPT)-O-3

- Major (MAJ)-O-4
- Lieutenant Colonel (LTC)-O-5
- Colonel (COL)-O-6
- Brigadier General (BG)-O-7
- Major General (MG)-O-8
- Lieutenant General (LTG)-O-9
- General (GEN)-O-10

Army Units

- Squad-usually led by a Staff Sergeant
- Platoon-usually led by a Lieutenant
- Company-usually commanded by a Captain
- Battalion-usually commanded by a Lieutenant Colonel
- Brigade-usually commanded by a Colonel
- Division-usually commanded by a Major General
- Corps-usually commanded by a Lieutenant General
- Field Army-usually commanded by a General

Army Staff Sections

S designates Army Staff Sections with organizations commanded by a MAJ-COL

G designates Army Staff Sections with organizations commanded by a General Officer

J designates a Joint (multi-service) Headquarters

- S/G/J-1: Personnel/Administration
- S/G/J-2: Intelligence/Security
- S/G/J-3: Operations
- S/G/J-4: Logistics
- S/G/J-5: Plans
- S/G/J-6: Signals/Communication
- S/G/J-7: Education/Training
- S/G/J-8: Finance
- S/G/J-9: Civil Affairs

Acknowledgements

My heartfelt thanks goes first to my husband who has believed in me and supported me throughout the years of writing this book. His insights and input to me in sorting out emotionally charged passages were invaluable. My first three editors were so important in forming my first rough draft into a book. First, Ananda Lo who was the first editor to help me organize my words into some semblance of coherent thoughts and to help define a theme. And to Alonzo who not only offered invaluable editorial advice on tightening my organization, but also gave me a male perspective and presentation ideas on my personal perspectives. Also, Rena Pacella, who first suggested I might have a broader audience than just my children (who I originally wrote for) and for guiding me to write for those readers. I must acknowledge my dear friends and family, Jen, Claudia, Mary, Joanne, and Yvette—It warmed my heart that you took the time to read my manuscript and provide feedback. And Bobby, who applauds everything that I do. Finally, I want to thank Tammy Letherer and all the people at Atmosphere Press who helped make my book a reality. You believed in me, my story, and my writing. You all have been invaluable to making this a product I am proud about and proud to share with the world. Thank you. Thank you. Thank you.

About Atmosphere Press

Atmosphere Press is an independent, full-service publisher for excellent books in all genres and for all audiences. Learn more about what we do at atmospherepress.com.

We encourage you to check out some of Atmosphere's latest releases, which are available at Amazon.com and via order from your local bookstore:

Finding Us, by Kristin Rehkamp

The Ideological and Political System of Banselism, by Royard Halmonet Vantion (Ancheng Wang)

Unconditional: Loving and Losing an Addict, by Lizzy and Adam

Telling Tales and Sharing Secrets, by Jackie Collins, Diana Kinared, and Sally Showalter

Nursing Homes: A Missionary's Journey Through Heaven's Waiting Room, by Tim Eatman Ph.D.

Timeline of Stars, by Joe Adcock

A Boy Who Loved Me, by Wilson Semitti

The Injustice in Justice, by Charmaine Loverin

Living in the Gray, by Katie Weber

Living with Veracity, Dying with Dignity, by Alison Clay-Duboff

Noah's Rejects, by Rob Kagan

A lot of Questions (with no answers)?, by Jordan Neben

Cowboy from Prague: An Immigrant's Pursuit of the American Dream, by Charles Ota Heller

Sleeping Under the Bridge, by Melissa Baker

The Only Prayer I Ever Have to Say Is Thank You, by M. Kaya Hill

Amygdala Blue, by Paul Lomax

About the Author

Roots and determination run deep for this woman. Serving at bases across America and abroad, she started out in the hard-working, blue-collar town of Buffalo. How was she to know that a child's fascination with her tight-lipped father's WWII Silver Star would begin an unexpected military career of 32 years starting as an enlisted soldier and rising to Army Colonel with a battle-field command?

Tougher than most, she went to Basic Training at 28; jump school at 38; and Iraq's war zone at 58.

All while raising five children, now successful adults, on her own. She has seven grandchildren and resides in Florida.

Made in the USA
Middletown, DE
16 November 2023